Faith Formers

Heroes of the Faith
Who helped others grow in their relationships with God

Written by members and friends of
Christians Engaged in Faith Formation (CEF)
In honor of CEF's 50th Anniversary

Edited by Patty Meyers, D. Min., Ed. D.

Christians Engaged
in Faith Formation

First published by Dog Ear Publishing
4011 Vincennes Road
Indianapolis, IN 46268
www.dogearpublishing.net

ISBN: 978-145756-649-3

This book is printed on acid-free paper.
Printed in the United States of America

Table of Contents

    East Highland Methodist Church, Columbus GA
    My Parents
    Mrs. Hogan
    Jill Beshell
    Jean Bowman
    Ruth Culpepper
    Rev. Ronnie and Julia Culpepper

Rev. Dick Reese
Margaret Greer
Dr. James Mickey Efird
Julia Bishop
Donna Slater
Jimmy and Joy Carr
Florence Jo Corban
Jimmy and Delia Dabbs
R. Harold Hipps
Donald Griggs

This book is dedicated to
the memory of R. Harold Hipps,
whose vision and efforts created a legacy
of Christian education,
faith formation,
and lifelong friendships,
to all the visionaries and saints who formed CEF,
and to all the people who have
formed us in our faith
and continue to do so today.

Foreword

This book honors the 50th anniversary of CEF, Christians Engaged in Faith Formation, formerly known as Christian Educators Fellowship. In it are essays of many persons who have helped the writers grow in their faith and become the people that they are today. The volume could surely have contained many more essays so readers are urged to consider and honor those who have formed their faith throughout their lifetimes.

This is a rich and inspiring collection of mini-biographies, much like a memoir. Most of those honored here are not the "rich and famous," but they are the stuff of legends. In fact, at the beginning of this project, its working title was "Legends." But *Faith Formers* more accurately portrays the important work of these saints.

The book is organized in sections: Family members, Sunday school teachers, ministers (whatever the demographic of persons with whom they served), professors and teachers, and "Village." Several essayists could not name just one or two important faith formers in their lives, so borrowing the African proverb, "It takes a village," the persons named in the "villages" appear in the Table of Contents and readers will find their names in **bold** font in the essays.

We are grateful to those who submitted contributions to this anniversary tribute. **CEF** would not be what it is today without these faith formers, nor would the essayists. The current CEF Board of Directors hopes that this volume will honor all

Christian educators, faith formers, and the unsung heroes of our faith.

Chamus Burnside-Savazzini
Lindsay Carter
Jennifer Finley
Tim Gossett
Scott Hughes, Discipleship Ministries
Jeff Lowery
Edward N. Ramsey
Victoria Rebeck, Higher Education and Ministries
Charmaigne VanRooyen
Patty Meyers, President, editor

Introduction

Christians Engaged in Faith Formation, formerly called Christian Educators Fellowship (CEF) began in 1968 with the dreams and commitment of some of those giants. R. Harold Hipps, Mildred Parker, Joe Zink and others put ten pennies in a small manila envelope and pledged to create an organization to support and encourage Christian educators, particularly those who work in local congregations. This book honors the visionaries who made a tangible pledge to start this organization in November, 1966.

Before that, in November 1965, a consultation on "relationships with local church Christian educators" was held in Cincinnati, Ohio. Out of that came a proposal for Christian education workers to be joined in one body and be known as Methodist Christian Educators Fellowship. Initially a steering committee gathered in Nashville, Tennessee in 1966. They constituted the Board of Directors of CEF in 1967.

1968 was a seminal year in the history of the people called Methodists. It was April 23, 1968 that the Evangelical United Brethren and the Methodist Churches united to form The United Methodist Church, the denomination out of which CEF grew. Even before that uniting conference, a charter of incorporation was signed on February 10, 1968 by the first executive committee of the CEF Board in Dallas, Texas: R. Harold Hipps, John N. Flynn, Mildred Parker, Mary Lou Van Buren, Joe T. Zink, Kendall W. Cowing. The charter was filed with the Secretary of State for the State of Tennessee. Its first conference was held October 28-31, 1968 in New Orleans.

The history of Methodist Christian education and faith formation can be traced back to the rectory of Susanna and Samuel Wesley, who insisted that their children be educated. While this book does not pretend to be a true history of CEF, in this 50th year of its existence, the current Board of Directors of CEF wanted to do something special in honor of the founding mothers and fathers of Methodist Christian education and Faith Formation.

Not only are the original group important, but so are the thousands of people who have served in numerous ways. There are many unnamed pioneers who left a legacy. They are all servant leaders. They are professors, directors and ministers of Christian Education, Sunday School superintendents, teachers, mentors, pastors, parents, grandparents and siblings. They are bishops, deacons, elders, but most lay persons.

Everyone stands on the shoulders of giants, giants that others may not know but who are very important to us. They are the faith formers, the ones who helped us become the people that we are today. Some of them have passed to the Church Triumphant; some are still living and inspiring today. They are mostly unknown and unsung heroes, but we couldn't do what we do if not for them.

The writers of these essays reflect The United Methodist Church in many ways. They are young and old, women and men, married and single, laity and clergy, from around the globe and close to home. They are volunteers and professional paid-staff persons. While not completely inclusive, the essays in this book were written by people who gave their time and attention to honoring important people in their lives. Thank you all!

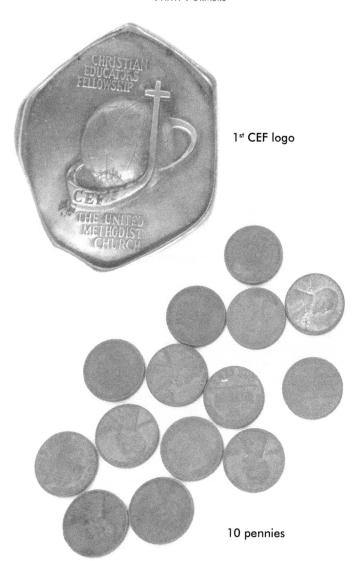

1st CEF logo

10 pennies

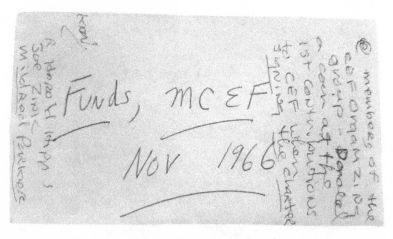

Outside envelope holding pennies, initial investment

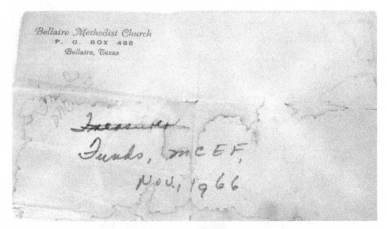

Inner envelope

1ˢᵗ charter signed

AN ACT OF HISTORY

The Charter of Incorporation of the Christian Educators Fellowship of The United Methodist Church, Incorporated was signed by the executive committee of the CEF Board of Directors on February 10, 1968. Those participating in the historical ceremonies at the Statler Hilton Hotel in Dallas, Texas, are shown in the photograph at the left. Seated are Chairman John N. Flynn and Secretary-Treasurer Mildred Parker. Looking on are R. Harold Hipps, CEF executive officer and representative from the Division of the Local Church, Board of Education; Mary Lou Van Buren, Member-at-Large; Joe T. Zink, Jr., Member-at-Large; Kendall W. Cowing, vice-chairman; Lena Mereness, representative from the Editorial Division, Board of Education. The Charter was filed with the Secretary of State for the State of Tennessee in Nashville on February 15, 1968. (Photo by Bob W. Smith of Dallas, Texas)

I.
Sunday school teachers

Sue Burman

I grew up in a small United Methodist church in the Chicago suburbs in the 1970's and 80's, Grace United Methodist Church in Elgin, Illinois. Over the years we were blessed by many wonderful pastors and Christian educators whom I could honor in this forum. However, as folks moved and leadership changed, there was one person whose influence and dedication was felt as a constant. Her name was Sue Burman. Sue was never on staff or paid for her work. She was a lay person and Sunday School teacher who loved children and wanted each and every child to know that God loved them. I remember well her positive upbeat attitude, how she joyously swayed back and forth when she sang, and her dedication to always be there for our Sunday School class.

As with much of ministry, what I remember most is not the content of the lessons that she taught but the ways in which she embodied the love of Christ in her relationship with her students. Sunday school was held before worship at Grace and the building was heated with radiators. Unless someone got up really early, Sunday school in winter time could be a cold affair. As we gathered for class in our coats and sweaters, Sue was always right there, teaching our small class as if we were a class of 50 with her sunny disposition warming us all. A second memory was when I was much older. I was a newly enrolled seminary student, trying to explore my emerging call from God. I helped start an afterschool tutoring program at Grace for the neighborhood children. We put out a call for folks to be tutors and were worried that we wouldn't get many volunteers

3

because of the age of our congregation. On the Sunday we made the announcement Sue was the first person to volunteer, which shouldn't have been a surprise. The children were again blessed to have her weekly presence in their lives for two years as we ministered to our neighborhood.

Sue was involved in ministry with children and families as far back as 1951 when she joined Grace church all the way up until the church closed in 2005. She was an example of the importance of consistency in ministry and had a profound impact on my faith and calling.

Jeff Lowery

Tim Gooch

I've been fortunate in my life to have people impact my faith journey, but the first person outside of my family to truly impact me was a Sunday School teacher named Tim Gooch. He taught my class when I was a junior in high school and was the first person to make faith not seem boring. He had no connection to my grade (his sons were several years younger), but he still decided to build into us. And build into us he did.

He was the first Sunday school teacher I had who treated us like real people, like young adults. He didn't have a theology degree (he worked in technology), but he knew pop culture. He taught a multi-week lesson on the theology of *The Matrix* trilogy, and took us over the railroad tracks to Dairy Queen a couple times. He let his personality shine through, even though his theology and politics (more often than not) differed quite a bit from that of the church leadership.

From his teaching I first learned that it was okay to think and believe differently. He engaged us in actual discussions and challenged what we thought we knew. There are still parts of those discussions that, even 15 years later, I can remember. Discussions about God as a pizza, debates on contemporary cultural issues, and general shenanigans still occupy warm places in my memory.

He once told us a story, and the story still forms a major part of how I minister. He was at a party once, in a group of people, some of whom he knew, some he didn't. At some point in the evening it had come up that he was a Christian, but at a later point he referenced the movie *Monty Python and the Holy Grail*, a decidedly un-Christian film. Years later, he occasioned to meet one of those people (with whom he was not friends) who mentioned to Tim that his *Monty Python* reference had caused him to re-examine Christianity. Because Tim had been himself, i.e., different, and showed that Christians could like non-Christian things, this random stranger came back to faith.

When I went on my Chrysalis flight as a high school senior, his letter was one of the ones that meant the most to me because, once again, he recognized that I was a young adult and real person who was on a faith journey. It also showed that he had paid attention to me in class, which I'm not convinced many of my other Sunday school teachers did. I even adapted his sarcastic and personal writing style for a letter I wrote for a student later in my adult life.

To this day, I remain in contact with him through the wonder of the internet. Like me, he has since left that local church, but maintains his faith and continues to check in on me and inform mine. I ran into him a short time ago at a local restaurant where he told me (in his typical, self-deprecating style), "Seeing your thoughts and posts online make me feel like maybe I didn't do a terrible job with you all." Far from it. He likely doesn't know the full extent of the impact he had on me, but I will always remember my time in that room.

Rusty Crimm

Minnie Lee Spencer and Dot Morse

Minnie Lee Spencer ("Min Lee") and Dot Morse were a dynamic duo in Sunday School at West Rockingham Methodist Church in North Carolina. They taught the nursery and primary classes and I was among their charges. Always arriving early in my crinolines* and black patent leather shoes, I immediately asked if I could help set out the story papers and Bible Verse of the Day. I remember these two women as being so kind and gentle and especially how they loved children and told us about Jesus.

Miss Spencer also directed the children's choir and taught us *Tell Me the Stories of Jesus*, and *The Little Brown Church in the Wildwood*, and *Into My Heart*. Miss Morse had a worship center that she changed every week. She would always bring in something interesting from nature—a rock or branch or flower -- and relate it to God. Both were widows I think, who in a small southern town shared their faith and their smiles with many children over the years. And let me tell you, those two could organize a Christmas pageant beyond comparison with sets and props and elaborate costumes. They went all out; we practiced for weeks!

I later found some of those story papers and started collecting old curriculum materials. They had a picture from a Bible story on the front and inside had the story and then some kind of learning activity. The resources were minimal back then and teachers had to rely on their own creativity and knowledge of the Bible. Being the over-achiever that I am, I memorized as many of the Bible Verses of the Day as my little head would hold (don't ask me to recite them all today). I can still remember the classrooms, one painted vivid blue and the little chairs. Did you have circle time in Sunday school? We did, of course. Miss Morse would tell us the Bible story, often in the voices of the characters, and ask us questions. My hand always shot up first, but she was careful to call on other children too!

You know for educators, there is usually a teacher or teachers that you can look back and say that person(s) influenced your vocation. Min Lee and Dot (as I called them later as an adult) were those teachers for me. I celebrate these humble servants who loved teaching and took great care with the little children. Curiously they seemed to know that we would amount to something someday.

Back then we had Promotion Sundays, and when I turned eight, I went on to another class, but Miss Spencer and Miss Morse will always be in my heart and soul.

- For the uninitiated, these were petticoats worn to make your dress stand out—standard fashion for little girls in the 1950s.

Susan Willhauck

Betty Jane Daniels Tilley (1936 -)

My mother has had the greatest and longest influence in my spiritual life and faith formation. I have known her all my life of course but it is through the last few years of my spiritual journey that I most see and appreciate her faith. She has remained a devout Christian my entire life. When I asked her if she grew up as a Christian she said that she did attend church from time to time with neighbors but it wasn't until she was in her late teens that she was saved, after marriage.

After marriage, she moved away from her home town to Iredell County NC where I was born and raised. She still attends the little church, which happens to be the same church that she raised me in, where I was saved and baptized, where my father attended as a child, and the church where his mother was raised.

My mother taught me the importance of faith, the importance of attending church, prayer, seeking God for guidance in my decisions, and to trust God. While she did not teach me to question God and the teachings in the Bible, she did teach me that no matter what I encountered in life that causes me to stumble and lose my way, that God will always love me and guide me to the answers I need through prayer or other ways. Even though I have rebelled and pulled away from God many times throughout my life, I have always believed in God and would pray for help and forgiveness and I attribute this mostly to my mother and my attendance in church as a child, thanks to her.

I attribute my faith and trust in God to the way my mother molded me from the time I was a little girl by always praying with me when she put me to bed and listened to me as I said my prayers. She often read scripture to me at night, and after tucking me in bed, she would say she was going to bed to read her Bible, which was a model for me to do the same as I grew older.

Another way that my mother has served a key role in my spiritual growth is through watching her not lose faith in God during times of great adversity. She never turned to drugs or alcohol, or cursing, or other things that many people do during hardships. She continued to pray and praise God for the better days to come. She managed to remain faithful to God, her church and her family even during times of crisis.

During the past five years I have experienced great loss and tragedy. I realize that my mother taught me to trust in God and that I must persevere. She has been my model to rely on God through pain and sorrow. While my circumstances may not turn around in the ways that I might desire or plan for myself, I need not dwell on my loss but have faith that God will design a new way for me so that I can be transformed and made whole again.

Phyllis Boyd-Van Hoy

Ray Zimmerman (c. 1935 - 2006)

Ray Zimmerman was my Sunday school teacher when I was growing up in Maryland. There were not many men who taught Sunday school in our congregation so I guess that he made a big impression on me. I wonder if he knows how much influence he had on my life and future profession. He was a beloved father and teacher.

Diana Hynson

II.
Parents, grandparents, other family members

Lessie Baldwin (1912-1980)

My faith has grown so much over the years; sometimes I am amazed at my personal and spiritual relationship with God. I never understood how a person could have such an in-depth relationship with God until I gained this relationship myself. Growing up in the south in one of the "Bible Belt" states (North Carolina), God and the church were a huge part of our upbringing. All my family members were active members of the church, whether it was being an usher, Sunday school teacher, or the preacher conducting Sunday morning worship. Even though I have been surrounded by "spiritually rich" individuals all my life, the main person that played a key role in my spiritual influence and faith formation is my mother.

My mother, Lessie Baldwin, was a proud and firm believer in God. Ever since I can remember she embedded in my siblings and me the importance of putting God first in our lives. She was born on September 10, 1912, in Ellerbe, North Carolina. My mother had the education of a sixth grader, but she gained her wisdom from her life experiences growing up in the segregated South. There is not a day that I did not see my mother giving glory to God, praising his name, or preaching and teaching God's word to my siblings and me. Every day was a day of worship in my household growing up, and she did not need anyone around to join her. Lessie did not force anyone's belief in God, but she had a good way of incorporating how God's presence in your life can be both beneficial and rewarding for mind, body, and spirit.

My mother's faith was so strong that even in the face of death she knew to lean on the Lord to get her through her pain and grief. During the time of my father's passing, my mother stayed in constant prayer and advised us to do the same. She told us that this was God's plan and no matter how much sadness, pain, or anger we felt, He had all the plans, and we must believe and trust in his plan. As I grew older and began to develop my relationship with God, all her advice, mentoring, and guidance became clear. I began to grasp a deeper understanding of staying in constant prayer, giving Him praise through the good and bad, looking to Him to help me through tough times, and the fact of just having a relationship with God that was necessary throughout my life and the lives of my children.

Lessie Baldwin passed away at the age of 75 on May 16, 1980. This was a day that I never prepared for, but because of her guidance, I did not hold anger or sadness; my spirit was at peace just as I knew hers was when she passed. I believe in my heart that she did not fight or object to God's angels to take her from this earth because she knew that it was God's plan. The way my mother lived her life and the morals and faith that she lived by had a major role in my spiritual formation. I do believe that without her reflection of faith throughout my life I would not truly know or understand the importance of God being at the center of my daily being.

Emma McKinney

Beverley Jean Fenner Buckingham
(1929-)

Jean Buckingham is my mother. Throughout my growing up in years, she served our home church as Church School Superintendent, President of the United Methodist Women, Chair of the Church Council, Chair of the Staff Parish Relations Committee, and many other offices. She also was employed for many years as church secretary. She began teaching Sunday school at age 17, and continued to teach into her 80's. She made sure that I got a solid Christian education both at home and at church, that I attended worship weekly beginning at the age of eight, and was active in MYF (Methodist Youth Fellowship). Her example of Christian faith, piety and leadership were incomparable.

When I was a child my mother read me stories of Jesus, John Wesley and Abraham Lincoln, her three heroes. She encouraged me to experience people and places different from those with whom and where I was familiar, to take on leadership roles in our church while a teenager, to take stands on the side of justice, to treat all people with dignity and respect.

In the early 1960's the city of Baltimore desegregated, and African Americans began moving into our neighborhood, and seeking to join our church. Most of the white members left. My mother, Jean, took on the then courageous role of welcoming our new neighbors into our church, while reassuring the older white members that all would be well, that we were all one in Jesus. She worked as a volunteer in our congregation for more than 65 years.

17

My mother's faith is the strongest I have ever known in anyone! Her sense of what God wanted – love and justice for all -- is and was invaluable and timeless.

Born in 1929, she still attends Sunday school at the age of 86.

Rick Buckingham

Claudia Crusell Buckingham

Claudia was my aunt by marriage. She earned a Christian education degree from Scarritt College in Nashville, and went on to serve as a Christian educator on staff at a church in Kenosha, Wisconsin. She met my uncle, Melvin Buckingham, at Scarritt. In 1951, she and Melvin were among the Methodist educators who met in conference at Estes Park, CO and suggested that there be a professional organization for them, an idea which came to formation in 1968 as CEF. She always encouraged me in my Christian commitment and educational calling.

I knew Aunt Claudia my entire life until her death. She was around I remember from an early age. A native of Georgia, she found herself in New Jersey, far from her family roots. Yet she loved me, her husband's nephew, as if I was a true blood relative. I visited her many times during her later years, first in New Jersey, and then in Georgia, where she modeled how to be gracious and accepting of coming old age without losing her Christian dedication and practice.

In the 1970's my aunt Claudia and uncle Melvin owned and operated a small hotel called "The Illinois" in Ocean City, New Jersey. At one point I was employed by them as a desk clerk, working long on-duty shifts. Whenever I had to work on a Sunday, she arranged my schedule to allow me to make it to church as I requested, and she encouraged the friendships I made there.

Claudia grew up very poor in rural Georgia. While her family had very little in material possessions, and she lost her father at a young age, they were spiritually rich in the sense if a strong faith that held them together. That surely must have influenced her faith formation, as she influenced mine.

Richard Buckingham

Melvin G. Buckingham

Melvin Guy Buckingham was my uncle. In the 1960's he owned and ran a private Christian day school called the Happy Hill School in McLean, Virginia. At the time of his death he was the Director of Christian Education (DCE) on staff at First United Methodist Church (later St. Peters UMC) in Ocean City, New Jersey. He gave me the example of a male Christian educator; he was a positive role model in a mostly female profession. His friends called him "Bucky." I knew him all my life, until his death.

He earned a Christian education degree at Scarritt College, then went on to serve as youth minister and/or Christian educator in various church settings, including one time the National Council of Churches. Christian education was his life's work.

My uncle Melvin encouraged me in my Christian commitment. He was a gentle soul who knew how to enjoy life in all of its fullness, and who encouraged me to make the most of the opportunities I had, which helped me to grow spiritually.

In 1966, when I was 16, my uncle and aunt took me with them to Expo '67, the World's Fair in Montreal, Quebec, Canada. It was my first trip without my parents. He trusted me with the freedom to explore; he respected me in conversation, and encouraged my adventurous spirit.

Melvin Buckingham was genuinely dedicated to his calling and his Lord. He had great stamina, but also knew how to enjoy life. He played the saxophone, called square dances, and generally brought joy to those around him.

He was a great mentor and role model for me and was a very strong influence on my personal and professional life.

Richard Buckingham

Annamae Burnside

In praise of Mother and Christian Schools:
Why I Believe what I Believe

I grew up in Freeport, Grand Bahama and was raised by Christian parents. I was raised with God at the center of everything I knew. I could recite the Apostles' Creed from start to finish from I when I was in the second grade, because it was mandatory at the Catholic School I attended. Everything I learned in that school and from my mother paved the way for what I would believe as I grew up.

I never thought about the words of the Apostles' Creed until I was studying for my first communion. There, Reverend Weir would ask us as a group, "Do you know why you come to church every week?" or "Do you know why we say the Apostles' Creed as Methodists?" Of course I did not fully understand but I knew I had to pass this class. As I looked back on this time in my life it seemed that nothing was connecting, I was just following the motions.

I went to a Methodist high school and we had a young educator who lead the Religious Education class and he was so energetic and what I would now describe as "fanatical" about why we should walk with God during our life journeys. As a high school student, I did not appreciate what he said, but as an adult I can never forget that he wanted us to invite God into our lives and live our lives as Christ did, not just go through the motions.

After being told what to do my entire young life, when I went off to college, I stopped going to church. I thought I just did not internalize what I was hearing. Learning was not enough for me, I needed to DO something in response to what I was being taught. After college a lady who was my senior, an employee of mine, invited me to church. At that first service I attended the pastor said, "Do not be a **spectator**, be a **participator** for God's glory." That was what I was missing, I was not using the skills and talents that God had given me for God's glory. So that day, I made a decision to start turning my life over to what God had prepared me to do: serve the church and serve the next generation. Even though I did not have children of my own, I believed that I was called to share the gospel of Jesus Christ with the next generation. I was not perfect, but I was willing because of what I believed.

Prayer: Dear Lord, I pray that you will continuously provide opportunities for me to turn my belief in to action all for your glory. Amen

Scripture: Matthew 25: 14-30

Chamus Burnside-Savazzini

Howard Caldwell (1931-2009)

My father, Howard Caldwell, was an alcoholic when I was two years old. While in rehab, he was in such bad shape that he died. In that state of "otherness," he remembered the main thing you hear about with a near-death experience. He talked about this glorious light that he desperately wanted to stay with but then he heard a voice. That voice said, "Howard, I'm not done with you yet." After that, God brought him back to the living and he was forever changed. Shortly after that he began the journey toward becoming an elder in the Methodist Church in upstate New York. Being raised by a person with such an experience is life altering. He showed me faith, kindness, empathy and an amazing way of connecting with people minus the judgment. He showed me light. He died nine years ago and I will be forever grateful.

He helped form my faith as he lived his faith out loud. He didn't just talk it. He showed it. He also made sure that I understood that there are different ways to accept Christ. Not everyone needs to be hit over the head with a near death experience. One way is not better or more significant than another. Thank God, he paid attention to the Voice of God!

In my father's first appointment as a student pastor (in his 40's) there was an angry older lady named Martha. No one liked Martha and many were afraid of her. I was in the 5th grade at the time. I told my dad that Martha wasn't a very nice person and that I didn't like her at all. He asked me if I really knew her. When I told him that I didn't, he said, "Don't you think you should try before you decide you understand her?" He then suggested that I go visit Martha after school one day. I thought this was a terrible idea, but I did it anyway. I even took her a few flowers as a gift. It didn't take long to realize that Martha was terribly lonely. She was delighted to have me visit and we struck up a great friendship. My father reminded me my whole life that you don't know someone until you know their story. He said that listening to people's stories was a spiritual practice, one that I never forgot.

He was a good pastor because God literally saved him. His ministry was always based on sharing the light of Jesus Christ. Especially in time of struggle. His empathy also made him able to reach people that others could not.

Laurie Hintz

William Stanley (Stan) Creighton

My husband is a genealogist and I just tag along most of the time. However, the task of writing family stories has fallen to me. I began with my father. One of my great treasures is a file drawer containing about 90% of his sermons. They span the 39 years of his active ministry as a deacon and then elder in The Methodist Church and The United Methodist Church, as well as a few from his seminary days, and most of those he preached in various churches during his 20 years in retirement. The majority of these sermons are in note form, rather than manuscript. As I have read them again and again, they have given me insight into my dad's life, as well as the persons who influenced him, the status of the world during his ministry, and how it was that he envisioned the kingdom of God.

For the most part when folks have inquired of me about my journey into ministry, I have named a college professor, **Nelle G. Slater**, as a primary impetus for my decision to become a certified Director of Christian Education. I wished to open doors to the Bible in the way she had opened it for me as we studied 'The Life and Teachings of Jesus.'

The months I have spent in careful study of my dad's sermons do not take away from her influence, but add a foundation that is broad and deep. It was through reading his sermons nearly 20 years after his death that I began to acknowledge his influence on the journey that led me to enter with joy the ministry of deacon with its focus on word, service, compassion and justice.

One of the great experiences of his life was appearing in a play, "The Unknown Soldier Speaks," based on a sermon by the same name which had been preached by John Haynes Holmes. With its focus on a world of peace, my dad performed the play over 80 times in camps, local churches and at a Methodist student conference in Evanston, Illinois in 1934. Said my dad many years later, "I felt as a Christian I was part of God's work for peace in the world." It was this focus of his life that has influenced much of my own thinking.

In 1997, less than a year before his death, my dad celebrated the 60th anniversary of his ordination as a deacon. Though he acknowledged that he could not sing (truer words were never spoken), he focused his sermon on the importance of ten hymns in reflecting his theology of social justice. I remember in one church a woman said as she left worship, "If we sing that hymn one more time, I'll scream." He did have a tendency to repeat the ones that were particularly meaningful to him. As a result the theology and social stance of these hymns became ingrained in me as well.

> *O help us stand unswerving against war's bloody way,*
> *Where hate and lust and falsehood hold back Christ's*
> *holy sway.[a]*
> *Spirit of God, descend upon my heart…Teach me to love*
> *Thee as Thine angels love.[b]*
>
> *Because He has anointed me to preach,[c] Go Tell it on*
> *the mountain.[d]*
>
> *We heed, O Lord, Thy summons, and answer Here are we!*
> *Thou canst use our weakness to magnify Thy power.[e]*

Once to every man and nation comes the moment to
*   decide...for the good or evil side.[f]*
That cause can neither be lost nor stayed
which takes the course of what God hath layed.[g]

Be strong! It matters not how deep entrenched the
*   wrong. Tomorrow comes the song.[h]*
To worship rightly is to love each other, each smile
*   a hymn, each kindly deed a prayer.[i]*

Grant us wisdom, grant us courage, lest we miss Thy
*   kingdom's goal.[j]*
*We **are** one in the Spirit.[k]*

How could I not respond to God's call to enter a ministry of word, service, compassion and justice?

a. O Young and Fearless Prophet – United Methodist Hymnal (UMH) No. 444

b. Spirit of God, Descend Upon My Heart - UMH No. 500

c. The Spirit of the Lord Is Upon Me - New Wine (no longer available)

d. Go Tell It on the Mountain - UMH No. 251

e. The Voice of God Is Calling - UMH No. 436

f. Once to Every Man and Nation - Book of Hymns (BoH) No. 242

g. That Cause Can Neither Be Lost Nor Stayed - 1938 Abingdon Song Book No. 239

h. Be Strong! - The Methodist Hymnal No. 300

i. O Brother Man, Fold to Thy Heart Thy Brother - BoH 199

j. God of Grace and God of Glory - UMH 577

k. They Will Know We Are Christians by Our Love –The Faith We Sing No.2223

Ann C. Bateman

Martha J. Davies-Sekle and Blamo L. Dueh

Martha J. Davies-Sekle (1925 – 1985)

Martha was born and raised in Freetown, Sierra Leone by her immigrant parents who migrated to Sierra Leone from Liberia. She was raised in the Catholic faith and was taught by her parents to be a faithful and devout Christian (Catholic). She came from a strong Christian background where her parents practiced their faith diligently.

She attended the University of Liberia graduating with a Bachelor of Arts degree in Communication. She later received her Master of Arts in Religious Studies from the University of Malta. She was the first female catechist in contemporary Africa and was given a dispensation by the Archbishop of the Catholic Archdiocese of Monrovia to administer Holy Communion.

She taught religious education at Saint Mary Catholic High School in Monrovia, Liberia for several years and catechism to young people who decided to embrace the Catholic faith until her passing.

She was an active member of the Legion of Mary and choir director for the choir at Our Lady of Lourdes St Mary's Parish. Her simplicity and humility was a source of inspiration for all those that came in contact with her both at work and at church. She was a woman of high values and virtues and these she did not hesitate to instill in her biological and adopted children.

Blamo Lewis Dueh (1969 -)

Blamo was born in Monrovia, Liberia to Nora Teah and Emmanuel Dueh. Even though his mother was a practicing United Methodist, Blamo was not raised in the Methodist faith because he was living with his father and stepmother who were both Pentecostals. He answered the call to ministry at the age of 17 during his last year in high school and became a faithful United Methodist.

Upon migration to the United States of America, he enrolled in the Charlotte Christian College and Theological Seminary where he obtained a Bachelor of Arts degree in Christian Education in 2016. He later entered Hood Theological Seminary where he is presently enrolled in the Master of Divinity program.

Blamo is a candidate for provisional elder in The United Methodist Church in the Western North Carolina Conference. He is actively involved in his local church (Hickory Grove United Methodist Church) and is presently serving on the program council and the evangelism team. He has served as assistant lay pastor for the African Ministry a worship venue for Hickory United Methodist Church that caters to Liberians in the diaspora.

His courage and boldness coupled with his love for God which is evident in his words and actions have become a source of inspiration for all those that come into contact with him. One of Blamo's favorite quotes from the Bible is Joshua 24:15: "As for me and my house we will serve the Lord."

Martha, who was my mother, was a source of guidance for me as I grew in my Christian faith. She was my early inspiration as a child. Blamo is my husband who introduced me to the Methodist faith and has had a significant influence on my faith also as an adult. His courage and boldness inspired me to step into my first leadership role in ministry as president of one of our United Methodist Women circles at our local church. I am thankful for how each of these individuals shaped me and continue to encourage me in faithful discipleship.

Sylvia Sekle-Dueh

Shirley Faulconer (1919 -)

The most influential person in my faith formation is my 98-year-old grandmother, Shirley Faulconer. She was born October 1, 1919 and resides in Culpeper, Virginia. Throughout my entire life she has always been a faithful follower of Jesus. In the past my grandmother served as a volunteer for her church by teaching Sunday School for many years and doing the clean up after communion, among many other things. For me though, it's how she lives out her life, and her actions in her home that have impacted me the most.

My high school years were some of the most formative in my faith journey. She didn't wait for me to ask questions, instead just involved me in her daily faith practices. Nothing staged or contrived, she would just share her Bible or devotion with me as she would be reading them. I never saw my mother or my father read a daily devotion or the Bible outside of church so this act had a great impact on me. She taught me how to love the Bible. As I grew, I started to share things I learned with her. I started reading Karen Kingsbury books and then giving them to my grandmother to read. I took Disciple Bible Study courses at my church and excitedly shared what I learned with her. Even today I talk passionately about my master's degree classes with her.

She's always been so open to sharing what she's learned from Sunday School classes or from her nightly devotional book. She talks about something new she's learned from a sermon or from Charles Stanley's nightly program. Just recently she talked about a new insight she had about what life was like for those supporting Jesus' ministry; how there had to be people that would take care of the cooking and cleaning where Jesus and the disciples stayed. She's still learning at 98 years young and that's inspiring to me.

My grandmother teaches me what strength is as she is the strongest person I know. She has endured so much loss. She's lost one daughter at age five, her husband, sisters, parents, a brother, and countless friends and relatives. She lost her other daughter, my mother, March 2016. Throughout the time my mother battled cancer, in her last days and the days that followed, my grandmother relied on Jesus. She asked for the pastor to come by to visit and pray with us in my mom's last days. There is no place I feel closer to God than at my grandmother's home.

Another lesson she taught me is forgiveness. There was a particular event within our family that deeply hurt my

grandmother and she talked to me about how she prayed to let go of the anger. She gave it to God and let it go.

My grandmother, Shirley Faulconer, lives for Jesus Christ. I am so thankful for her example of faith for without it, I don't know if I would be the person in Christ that I am today. I only pray that I can be as strong, passionate, loving and godly as my grandmother is.

Stephanie Jenkins

Gertrude and other Grandmothers

There was a time that I was afraid to tell people my middle name, Arlena. I thought it sounded too old fashioned and mountain-like, although I was born in the beautiful mountains of Asheville, North Carolina. What do kids really know anyway? Some of the things we think are important pale in comparison to God's expansive desire to love us.

While my parents were the main reason for my religious experience, there were others in my community village that assisted in my *spiritual* development. I give that credit to my Grandmother Lena, my Grandmother Pauline and our next-door neighbor – 'Grandmother' Gertrude. My parents were very vocal and authoritative about God's word and law, but my grandmothers were great examples because of the fruit they exhibited and their service extension in the community. My grandmothers had a huge influence on my life. The seeds of stewardship, servant-leadership and civic responsibility were planted from conversations and experiences I had with these community lights.

Grandmother Lena, from my paternal side, always had family, neighbors, church members and community leaders coming to visit and recline on the porch for rich authentic conversation. She kept fresh vegetable dishes and rich delectable desserts on the table. Looking back, I wonder how the polar opposites of food seemed to put everyone in an insatiable trance from the savory smells steeping through the window of the dining room flowing right onto the porch. I enjoyed sitting at her feet, while she braided my hair, and listening to the testimonies of faith, sorrows of life and the joys lives living in obedience to God. Grandmother Lena's knowledge of scripture and hymns could hold its own weight against any of the knowledge from the medical doctor's, whose homes she cleaned in the wealthy Biltmore Forest community.

My Grandmother Pauline, my mom's mother, encouraged me -- more than any other family member -- to be myself. She always knew that I was unique and invited me to be my authentic self. Whenever my parents scolded me in Grandma Pauline's presence, she'd send a sharp reply back to them to "leave me be." That warmed my heart and made me feel so accepted. Her unconditional love modeled grace in a way that was loving and Christ-filled. Visiting her during the summers in Lake Lure, NC made my summer vacation all the sweeter.

In order to escape the demands of helping to raise my sisters and brothers and the big expectations of being the oldest, I would often retreat to some private spots that I discovered to refuel and make sense of life. One of those sacred spaces included the weeping willow tree in "Grandma Gertrude's" back yard. Gertrude Graham didn't have any children of her own, but she tenderly adopted all of the neighborhood children, who gave her the affectionate name of "Grandma Gertrude." She was a retired teacher who extended her love of teaching to us. We'd spend a couple of afternoons in her backyard, learning the art of crocheting, painting and other crafty projects. Classical and jazz music streamed through her living room windows to our yearning ears in the art studio of her backyard. Grandma Gertrude always coupled the lessons with biblical insights and practical nuggets for living. She exuded the engaging fellowship of community koinonia more than anyone I could remember.

I am truly grateful for all of my grandmothers, and embrace my middle name more than ever now.

Sherry Arlena Waters

My Dad

After my parents split up when I was a kid, my father started to get very involved in church and rediscovered his own faith, which helped me to discover my own faith. He was very encouraging and knowledgeable having grown up in the church himself. He imparted a lot of the wisdom about what it means to be a follower of Jesus to him and what that look like practically not just being a Christian but living as one. He was very knowledgeable, dedicated and loving, a good role model.

Kevin Clipel

Ed. Note: This essay was transcribed from an interview at the 2016 CEF Conference in Nashville. It was hard to hear so if the author's name is not correct, please accept this apology. Honoring one's father is not only biblical but a good witness to others.

Tacy (1903-1975) and Wilbur (1902-1972) Schappert

Tacy and Wilbur were the pillars of the church in which I grew up in Cedar Rapids, Iowa. They were lay persons, not clergy. Tacy was my childhood Sunday school teacher. Wilbur taught the adult Bible study. They sang in the choir and played in the band. Their children were mostly grown-up and their hearts seemed to expand for others. I called them Gram and Gramps though we were not biologically related. They both instilled in me a love of the Bible. They helped form my faith in God and helped it to expand as I grew.

In addition to their service at the church, they were caregivers for my family. Whatever my parents knew about parenting they learned from Tacy and Wilbur. They were generous with their time, their home, and other resources. They provided child care and support for my siblings and me in numerous ways. Wilbur taught me that men could be kind and gentle, that they could listen and wipe away tears instead of causing them. Tacy taught my mom to crochet the most beautiful beaded doilies and how to braid hair. At the end of the day I loved to watch Tacy take down her braids that she kept wrapped in a bun and brush her soft gray hair.

My mother said that Tacy decided the day I was born that I had the fingers of a pianist, and so I did. She and Wilbur gave me my first piano when I was five years old. I've never been without a piano and have been a church musician most of my life, starting at age 9. I started teaching Vacation Bible School at age 14. They modeled faithfulness to God, to each other, their family and all God's children. Because I found such comfort on their back porch swing, I have always had one in my homes. I even named my beloved Chihuahua Tacy; if it had been a boy, its name would be Wilbur. It's a small way of holding them close.

I could tell many stories about them. I have only one photograph of them, taken Easter Sunday 1969, which I keep near my desk to look at every day. They were both "promoted to glory" – as they say in The Salvation Army -- in the early 1970s but I shall never forget them. They were very important to my faith formation and my development as a woman of God. Neither they nor their children likely knew how important they were to me, but their faithfulness is legendary.

Patty Meyers

Louise S. Talbert (1949-2009)

Louise S. Talbert is the person who most influenced me in my faith formation. I always knew she was special but I did not realize her full impact until I began my journey into ministry. Although I was ordained as a Baptist minister in 2017, it was in her womb that that my faith formation journey began. My grandmother told me that I was ordained over forty years ago when my father was ordained as a deacon. During my father's ordination, my mother was seven months pregnant with me. It is my grandmother's belief that I was ordained in that ceremony too.

My mother was very active in the church. Over the years she held numerous roles at the church where she faithfully served. She was such a Godly woman that she allowed her light to shine in all aspects of her life. Ma is what we called her. She always had a kind word and always helped others. Ma was a sickly woman for the majority of her adult life. She battled with lupus as well as heart problems which required the use of a pace maker after the birth of my youngest brother. These health problems never stopped her from serving.

I believe that she served herself to death. I remember seeing her sick and serving at the same time. She had a younger brother who suffered from cerebral palsy and required around the clock support. After Ma's mother passed in 1988, she made it her duty to take care of her disabled brother. She had brothers who were supposed to be his "care givers" but somehow she ended up caring for her brother more than the "care givers" did. Along with taking care of her brother, working as a teacher and school bus driver, caring for her husband and three sons, she continued to serve in the church.

Ma was a praying woman; she had to be because she had three knuckle-headed boys. She once told me that she prayed extra hard for her boys because she was concerned about their souls. My mother recognized her genealogy and the potential of her boys to become hustlers, gamblers, and drunkards. She said that she would pray, "Lord please save my boys before they leave this earth." The Lord allowed her to see two of her sons become deacons and the other a church trustee.

In late December 2012, she was diagnosed with stage four pancreatic cancer. The doctor gave her four months to live; Ma left this world in three. When given the death sentence, she did not flinch but my brothers and I cried like babies. She did not flinch because she had a peace that surpassed all understandings. She demonstrated that peace because of her faith in her salvation. Seeing this also helped with the formation of my faith.

On her death bed, I was able to witness true servitude. When she was well, Ma loved cooking and serving. In her transitional stage she experienced delusions and hallucinations; she tried to serve food to the people waiting around her deathbed. She told my father, "Albert, don't just stand there, fix them a plate." This act showed me that if she can have the audacity to serve on her deathbed then I can serve in my present state of health. My mother, Louise S. Talbert helped form my spirituality by displaying an undying love for serving.

LaVictor R. Talbert Sr.

Sarah W. Wood
(1957 – Still here with us!)

When I think back on my relationship with Christ, I can most certainly say that a leader in my life and example for me was my mother, Sarah W. Wood. She was the person who most influenced my faith formation. She was the cornerstone in my life in general but she was also a great example for who and what a Christian person should be and how to live their life. There are many moments that I remember thinking, "this is a really hard time," but she remains steadfast in her belief that God is here with us and providing for us and that despite the curve ball that has been thrown, God will get us through it.

I can remember from a very early age that our going to church on Sunday mornings was very important, and not just to worship but to Sunday school as well. This was hard for some people to understand, especially as my mom is a cardiac care nurse at WakeMed and at the time worked every other weekend. But still on the weekends that she was home we were dressed and at church ready for Sunday school and then worship, then home. Mom was also active in her own Sunday school class and then, in stages, would help teach Sunday school for the children's ministry. This helped set the stage for me wanting to be able to give back and to help others, as my mom was doing.

Despite having a husband who traveled every week for work and two children participating in different sports and scouting activities, my mom was also a member of Bible Study Fellowship, which is an in-depth Bible study where many women meet once a week to speak about and learn more about the Bible. Mom would use the time in the afternoon when my brother and I were doing our homework, to do her BSF homework. I remember thinking that I wanted to be that devoted to God and that when I did homework, it could be learning more of the Bible instead of multiplication tables of the differences in verbs, adjectives and pronouns. Those afternoons were filled with the sounds of a Christian radio station and once homework was done, after dinner, we always shared devotions and read the Bible. In car rides she encouraged us to listen to Christian songs and to sing along, to learn the promises of Jesus.

My mother's father passed away when I was in sixth grade and I remember how hard that was to watch her and to experience my own grief for my Papap. The strength that my mom showed, the comfort and peace that God gave her in saying goodbye to her Daddy, gave me a strength that one day I would experience as well. God was right there with my mom in those moments, she never let me see her doubt God. She promised that God was there with us and assured us that Papap was there with God as well. She shared this verse with me, "For our light and momentary troubles are achieving for us an eternal glory that far outweighs them all. So we fix our eyes not on what is seen, but on what is unseen, since what is seen is temporary, but what is unseen is eternal." (2 Cor 4:17-18).

In the past year and a half since my dad's death, my Mom has been here each step of the way, not only dealing with her grief, but mine and my brother's. Whenever we start to feel down, she constantly reminds us to claim what Jesus has taught us and promised us, that Jesus is right here with us and that he is asking us to share his love, just as she does.

Sarah Wood

III.
Ministers

A Minnesota Story

Several wonderful CEF'ers to whom I owe an enormous debt of gratitude shaped my journey to ordination. To this day I remain so very grateful for the ways in which they shaped not just my ministry, but me as a person of faith.

I have always felt a call to ministry; I just didn't have a way to express it. When I started taking my children to Sunday School and they had questions I couldn't answer, especially ones about forming faith, I didn't know where to turn. Then I heard about "CEF." I got in my car (and always seemed to get lost, since in those days I didn't drive much further than church, Target and National Guard duty!) and made my way to a meeting. The people of this organization took me in and began to shape and form me.

Who are these awesome folks? They're all retired now and some have gone home in the arms of Jesus.

Sally Wizik Wills –She taught me so much I can't name it all, but most especially I'm grateful for learning how to choose curriculum and later how to implement The Rotation Model.

Joan Lilja and Dandy Lewis – From them I learned so very much about children's ministry, but I also learned how to plan and carry out a day camp. They were such fun and gracious co-workers and friends. Their good grounding allows me to still lead camps for kids today.

Corrine Van Buren – Corrine came along side me when I experienced a very personal crisis moment. I don't know if she even remembers it, but it's like yesterday to me and I'm so grateful for her wisdom and care. She helped me make a difficult decision that changed the very course of my life!

Chris Jackson – He taught me to name and claim not just my ministry, but also my place in it. I can still hear him say, when I had questions, "*The Book of Discipline* says SHALL, not maybe or if you want to…).

Jane Souhrada – She is now gone from this earth, but she was an early mentor who literally taught me that my call began at baptism and is shaped by that water every single day.

Jan Pettit – I remember her gentle presence as she led our CEF meetings and retreats. Oh, how I wanted to be like her! What a gracious and kind person she was. I cherish her memory. We celebrated her life on this just recently but her presence is forever remembered.

To each of these I can only a wholehearted thank you. From each of these I learned the value of CEF for that I will always be grateful.

Cindy Yanchury

Leon Eugene Adney (1929-2010)

Major "Gene" Adney was a native of Wisconsin who served as a pastor for 58 years in The Salvation Army in Wisconsin, Iowa, and Michigan. He was married to Yvonne, who became my mother's best friend. Even after he retired he continued to do volunteer service for The Salvation Army. He also was active in Kiwanis for many years.

Major Adney liked to work with his hands. He'd been a farmer before going to the Salvation Army Training College. He liked to fish; it was a good way to relax. He really loved being a pastor. He liked to help people and I was one of those people he helped. He was a big man physically and spiritually. Although he worked hard in the congregations he served, (he was assigned to the corps in Cedar Rapids, Iowa where my family worshipped when I was a boy), he made time for the things that he thought were important, like kids and fishing. When I moved to Wisconsin, I attended the corps that he served there.

It was the time he spent just with me one-on-one that had the greatest influence. My parents always had a rocky marriage, to say the least, that ended when I was nine. Major Adney was a strong, stable influence in my life when everything seemed chaotic. I could count on him in ways that I couldn't count on other people. He got me through some really hard times throughout my life. Even when he was no longer officially my pastor, he didn't relinquish that role for me. He showed me what a good man could be. He pulled out his Bible and showed me the words of eternal life. He had a way of putting things in simple language that made sense to me, not that I always followed his counsel, but he was "there" for me.

Major Adney was a preacher, a teacher, a surrogate dad, a counselor, and a good role model. He did more to help form my faith than anyone.

R. Kevin Haley

Cay Barton (1961-2013)

Cay helped me in my faith journey by sometimes leading, sometimes following, but she was always close by, helping me see the face of God through her activities. I was never the "perfect" Christian but I was always well-armed and loved by Cay over the 15 years I knew her.

Cay and I lead a covenant discipleship class for 5th graders and a prayer class for 4th graders. Through my life's ups and downs, Cay was always there to remind me that ours is a loving and graceful God.

Sometimes working with children and parents can be stressful. Cay helped me to see all sides of conversations. I witnessed her patience and kindness that always reflected her open heart and mind with children and grown-ups. Cay was an expert at building relationships. She had a way of knowing what individual children needed and how to meet those needs.

Cay served 25 years as a Children's Minister on her church staff. She was an important person who influenced my life.

Author Unknown

Ann Bateman (1943 -)

I have known Ann for at least 40 years. Ann's primary influence occurred during her years as my candidacy mentor. Her influence arrived through her steadfast support and modeling of servant ministry. My route to service and justice was a bit rugged and LONG.

Ann's ministry in Christian Education had also been my goal when I was a diaconal ministry candidate. I loved using experiential learning such that Thomas Groome taught and which Ann practiced beautifully. Walter Wink's biblical study methods were also instrumental in her work and mine.

However, once I was pulled toward advocacy and justice work following a life altering United Methodist Church trip to Nicaragua in 1982, there were consequences. My organizing/ coordination efforts with the Fellowship of Reconciliation were opposed within my local church, and this reality threatened my candidacy.

Ann drove to Central Oregon and advocated on my behalf with the Council on Ministry. More importantly, she spoke to the role of professional diaconal ministry within The United Methodist Church. Her support encouraged me to trudge on. I was likewise guided by the Christian base community (liberation theology) we were building through our FOR.

Her patience and then mine, did lead to the spiritual growth I needed to carry on in ministry. Knowing Jesus as a companion with the poor and oppressed was deepened and secure.

Later appointed at the regional level of Habitat for Humanity International, I returned to practice forms of Christian education: creating, presenting countless workshops, trainings, retreats, and worship in large conferences. Throughout my ministry I often reflected with the question, "How would Ann do this?" I also imagined her calm, firm presence during the occasional difficult Habitat situation. The Holy Spirit once more abideth with me.

Ann was a Diaconal Minister for many years, then became a Deacon in Full Connection. She served as a self-employed appointed church consultant and on staff with the Corvallis Oregon First UMC. She usually met with me at our Suttle Lake Camp in the Oregon-Idaho Conference, more than halfway between her home and mine. Her work began in Southern California, then moved to Oregon, where she has served in many leadership capacities and has served beyond the bounds of the annual conference; she has been a delegate to Jurisdictional and General Conference.

Ann is loved by many, as she loves us.

Annis Henson

Mildred (Millie) Sunshine Cooper
(1921-2017)

Millie Cooper was one of the many saints that helped guide my faith formation as a youth. Having moved from North Carolina to Roanoke, Virginia, I first met Millie at a Virginia Conference Youth Rally. She embodied the personality of a "pied piper," gathering young people around her wherever she went. She helped youth connect with each other and with the adult leadership (clergy and laity) in the conference.

She was a mainstay throughout my high school and college years, and I maintained a relationship with her into my adult years, keeping her up to date with my personal, family, and professional rites of passage. We often shared letters and Christmas cards.

Millie saw in me gifts, graces, and talents that were raw, but had potential. She affirmed me and she guided me. She was the first person to question me on my potential call to ministry and found ways for me to experience roles of leadership. She was the first adult to encourage me to examine a call to the ministries of Christian education. As a teenager, I served on the Virginia Conference Council on Youth Ministry and I was given opportunities to serve on the Conference Social Concerns Committee and on the planning/design teams for youth events at Blackstone Conference and Retreat Center and Camp Alta Mons. I served as a youth delegate to three Virginia Annual Conference Sessions and as one of two Youth Delegates from Virginia to the 1976 Southeast Jurisdictional Conference.

During my senior year in high school, Millie asked me to serve, not as a youth participant, but as the co-chair (with an adult) of the planning committee for an annual conference youth mission project. Her trust in me and belief that I could do it had a profound effect on me.

Beginning in 1968, Millie served on the Virginia Conference Staff as the Director of Youth Ministries. She was a Diaconal Minister, and introduced me to the ministry of the laity in the areas of Christian Education ministries. Millie retired in 1984 but stayed active in youth ministry until 1988.

Millie was a graduate of Newport News High School, Peabody College for Teachers, and Scarritt College. She held positions at Ginter Park Methodist Church (Richmond), Chestnut Avenue Methodist Church (Newport News), Monumental Methodist Church (Portsmouth), and Arlington Methodist Church (Arlington) before joining the Virginia

Conference staff as Youth Director in 1968. She worked with all ages, but truly loved working in Christian education with youth. Millie loved all people and was loved by them in return.

David Melton

Teresa Dunn (1969 -)

One of the biggest influences in my life and someone who has helped me develop my spirituality and form my faith is Teresa Dunn. I have known Teresa since 2006, when I first entered my youth group at Providence United Methodist Church in Charlotte, North Carolina.

Teresa Dunn has been the Director of Youth and College Students for more than 15 years at Providence. Teresa was born in 1969 and she didn't start off wanting to work in the church. Teresa wanted to have a career in dance. She did not go off to college right after high school but instead stayed home and helped teach at a dance studio while pursuing a dance career. At the same time, she did volunteer work in a church. It did not take long until she started to pursue her vocation in ministry. Teresa found her way to Providence UMC in 1998 and I eventually found myself wanting to become involved in the youth group at Providence. That's when our worlds collided.

I knew from the first year I met Teresa that she was going to be someone important in my life while being a youth at Providence. I learned to be honest with myself and how to seek God's will for my life. I learned a lot about my faith from Teresa, including how to have a close relationship with God as well as how to sit down and read the Bible. After my seven years in youth group and my graduation from high school, my relationship with Teresa didn't stop. Her influence in my life and on my faith continues to this day.

The beginning of my college experience was not perfect and I definitely turned my cheek to God and wasn't always the best Christian I knew I could be. Through all of this I knew that I could still talk to Teresa and go to her in my weak moments. I often felt comforted by her words and guidance.

The summer between my junior and senior year of college, I interned with the Providence youth under Teresa's guidance. In three short months I learned a lot, including how to be confident in my faith, how to be persistent in it even when it is difficult and how to be independent in my faith. When I was in the youth group my faith was mainly based on those around me. It was harder for me develop my faith on my own but Teresa helped lead me to learn how to do that. Now, three years later, I am working under Teresa's guidance, doing youth ministry at Providence, and I continue to learn from her. She continues to push me in my faith formation and spiritual development. Through all these years I have always been able to look to Teresa for guidance and help when I struggled in my faith. She has always been there to help push me through the obstacles I've faced. Teresa Dunn has been the biggest and longest influence in my life. She has been with me through many different stages in my life and I know she will continue to do so in the future as well. She is minister, mentor and friend.

Olivia Tobin

Esa, Mother, Warren and Isabel Light, and Barbara Nixon

My faith was inspired by many people. First was the first pastor I can remember. Her name was **Esa** and she was part of the United Church of Christ in Ione, Oregon. She used unconventional practices in this small town, including chimes for meditation and her husband was a Native American Spirit Guide who would tell stories from his culture. When I was about six years old, I said, "Goodbye God" as I was leaving the church and waving at her. She was concerned and asked my parents if we could have a chat after church the next week. We sat in a corner and spoke very intensely for most of the coffee hour. When I left the church I promptly turned around and waved again saying, "Goodbye God." She rolled her eyes and looked at my parents saying, "At least she got the gender right." She taught me that God could be in people and that women could lead a church with more than the Bible.

Second and more constantly is **my mother**. She continued to teach me that faith is more than Christianity. She believes in reincarnation and karma. She could never meditate but never stopped me from meditation and yoga. We have many discussions on the different points of different faiths and how they change the way we see the world. She also taught me that God is always listening and I didn't need to be in an attitude of prayer to talk to God. I continue to talk to God when I am driving about what I need or don't understand in the world like I would my parents when I was younger, as if God is in the car seat next to me. The other thing she allowed was to be angry with God. I have had my fights with situations in my life I don't understand. We have a family tradition of having a list of questions to ask God when we arrive in heaven. When I am so angry at my current situation I am stuck, I often will add a question to God to my ever growing list.

More recently my pastors have been my faith formers. I stepped away from the church when I was in college because I was trying to find myself and church had been the family business. However, I did attend the Wesley Center at the University of Oregon because they always had a free meal and a good conversation with old friends. That is where I met **Rev. Warren and Isabelle Light.** I was skeptical because I grew up in a very conservative small town. College had allowed me to rebel a bit and I did that by joining the "Rocky Horror Picture Show" shadow cast at the University of Oregon. I played Eddie. I set up a challenge. I told the Lights about my part of the Rocky Horror Picture Show and expected them to have the normal conservative response of taking a breath and grabbing their pearls, but they didn't pause for a second. They immediately told me how much they liked the show and that they had their prop bags ready. It told me that I could really be myself at church and I would be accepted rather than told to be more conservative.

Finally, my current pastor **Rev. Barbara Nixon**. I was skeptical when I first met her knowing what I did about The United Methodist Church's inner workings. As a bisexual person, I was hurt by my church's stance on LGBT community. However, Barbara has helped me to grow my faith through small group workshops and the pastor's forum where we talk about the service every week. I came in thinking "God has a plan" and I realized as time when on that this had become a passive phrase for me where I didn't need to take action because God would. Barbara taught me that God is asking me to take part and that I can make the world better. So rather than asking God why would they do this in my world I can stand up and be a part of the change because that is what God is asking me to do.

Courtney Nelson

William Franklin Graham Jr.
(1918-2018)

Born in Charlotte, NC to William and Morrow Graham, William Franklin Graham received a Bachelor's of Science in Theology from the Florida Bible Institute and attended Wheaton College for further instruction. This is where he met Ruth McCue Bell and they were married on August 13, 1943.

Graham first pastored at First Baptist Church in Western Springs, Illinois, before leaving to join Youth for Christ which was an evangelical movement that ministered to servicemen returning from World War II as well as young people. It was not long before it became evident to Billy Graham and those around him of his gift in proclaiming the truth of God's Word. In 1950, the Billy Graham Evangelical Association (BGEA) was formed, which created a platform for Billy Graham to minister to people worldwide. Through the BGEA, Graham could proclaim the Gospel to as many as 215 million people over 185 countries and has preached to more people than anyone else in history.

Early on in his ministry, he was challenged by someone questioning the authority of the Bible. Better known as "the tree stump prayer," Graham set his Bible on a tree stump and said to God, "There are many things in this book I do not understand. There are many problems with it for which I have no solution. There are many seeming contradictions. There are some areas in it that do not seem to correlate with modern science. I can't answer some of the philosophical and psychological questions Chuck and others are raising...Father, I am going to accept this as Thy Word—by faith! I'm going to allow faith to go beyond my intellectual questions and doubts, and I will believe this to be Your inspired Word!"[1] This became the turning point in his life of ministry.

I first encountered the ministry of Billy Graham during his Charlotte Crusade of 1996. I was 16 years old then and attended this crusade with my youth group. I would say that this was my first awareness of God's prevenient grace and the first time I can recall hearing with fresh ears that Jesus Christ was the Savior. Being raised in church, I am sure the name of Jesus as spoken before, but this time it was different. His name began to sink into my spirit rather than merely my head. And just like Billy Graham's "tree stump prayer" I began soaking myself in God's Word to learn more about who Jesus was. The seeds of faith had been planted but did not bear fruit until November 7th, 2012, when I finally made the connection that Jesus was not just *the* Savior, but was *my* Savior, in what Wesley would call justifying grace. In that moment, I began a restored relationship with God the Father through His Son Jesus Christ and later learned that November 7th is Billy Graham's birthday.

Finally, in 2013 I had the privilege of working for BGEA in the Christian Response Department. While there, every day I would pass by a picture of Billy Graham during his South African Crusade with a caption of "Go into all the world…" and every day I passed by this, I felt a sense of God's call on my life to "Go into all the world…" Sitting here today, I cannot fully articulate what this call of God is yet but what I do

---

[1] https://billygraham.org/story/the-tree-stump-prayer-where-billy-graham-overcame-doubt/

know is Billy Graham has played a significant part in my faith formation.

Billy Graham will turn 100 this November 7th and will stand as the best evangelist of all time because he took God at His Word and simply believed that God had a purpose and a plan for his life far beyond anything he could have created himself. He simply believed God and when it comes down to it, this is what God is calling me to do, to simply believe regardless of what I can or cannot see.

Carri Killian

Ed. Note: Graham died after this essay was submitted so the year 2018 was added.

Dale Hanaman

My parents were family camp directors each summer at a church camp in Wisconsin, so they would get regular reports about the registration statistics at all of the church camps in my conference. The summer before my freshman year in high school, I made a life-changing decision. After studying the numbers, I decided to sign up for clown camp. Why? There were thirteen girls signed up and no boys. Perfect, I figured!

The camp was far more fun than I anticipated it would be. While the male/female ratio the next three years was never quite as good as they were that first year, I made many great friends and learned skills that would last me a lifetime.

Clown Camp was directed by Rev. Dale Hanaman, a United Methodist pastor from the Wisconsin Conference. Dale looked like Grizzly Adams, with a giant greying beard and long, full, wiry hair, and I would have guessed he normally rode a Harley. His demeanor, though, was quite the opposite of his grizzled appearance. He was gentle, soft-spoken, and always fully present.

Our daily routine included a trip to a location near the camp where we could "clown around," dressed in whatever clown gear we had brought with us, our faces painted with the clown makeup provided by Dale. We visited hospitals, retirement centers, parades…anywhere our presence would spread a little joy. I learned to make balloon animals, improved my juggling abilities, and got inspired to eventually learn fire eating. (If Dale could do it with that beard, I figured anyone could!) Most importantly, I learned how to visit with people who really needed a bright spot in their day.

During the evening, we debriefed our day together, and this was the aspect of camp that has stuck with me the most as a Christian educator. Dale gave us notebooks and daily questions to reflect on, such as, "Where did you find joy today?" or "What did you learn about yourself?" We wrote in silence for a long time, then shared some of our answers with the group. This was truly a holy moment in our day, and it was a kind of faith formation I had never experienced before.

Clowning is not a quiet activity, generally. For an introvert like me, it can be difficult to sustain that level of energy throughout the day. Our debriefing times gave us space to reflect, an opportunity to listen to the still small voice within, and to process our experiences in community. I have been to dozens of terrific church camps, but the environment Dale created was like no other, and it has informed much of what I do in Christian education now. Our lives today are so busy and the distractions are numerous, which is why I think the model Dale demonstrated for us is probably even more relevant now than ever.

It would be fair to say that Dale planted a seed that eventually grew into my call to full-time youth ministry. His camp gave me the first look at a way of doing youth ministry that was about creating memorable experiences and connections, not about crazy lessons, pizza, and lock-ins. Incidentally, when I accidentally bumped into Dale at Annual Conference recently, I learned that he retired and moved from northern Wisconsin to a town less than an hour from me in Iowa! I'm hopeful that there will be many more opportunities to be in his presence, to reminisce about camp, and maybe even to eat fire together too!

Tim Gossett

Chris Lynch (1973 -)

Chris Lynch serves as a congregational specialist in the Rock Hill district of the South Carolina United Methodist Conference while he also leads the entire conference's Ministries with Young People but I'll always know Chris as my youth pastor. Chris had an incredible impact on my walk with Christ and went above and beyond to show me how important a caring adult can be in the life of a teenager. I can tell of many stories that illustrate this but there's one story that sticks out to me the most.

When I was nine years old, my parents came to talk my younger sister and me to tell us that they were getting divorced. We were both crushed. We knew families that went through divorce and the bouncing around that kids do and we saw that in our future. We knew our parents' relationship wasn't perfect but we also thought they held it together pretty well. As time wore on and they "repaired" things, this conversation took place almost every year and the relationship remained fractured. On Thanksgiving Day when I was in middle school, my parents got into a huge argument and as typically happened, it turned physical. Unlike their other arguments though, they both decided to independently take action and called the police to report each other for domestic violence. As we all quickly discovered, you cannot rescind an allegation of domestic violence once the police arrive. It makes sense, the victim could be threatened to take back what they said. Since both of my parents had accused the other of domestic violence, the police took both to jail and left me as a 12 year old and my younger sister as an 11 year old home alone on Thanksgiving Day. My older sister had been off to college for a few years and was with her fiancé's family and my grandparents had recently moved to Florida.

My mother made the decision to call Chris Lynch. I am not sure what prompted that call and I have never asked her why she decided to call him. As a father of two young girls, one a very recent newborn (who is now in my youth group as a ninth grader), Chris left his family on Thanksgiving Day to come get my sister and me. He took us back to his home, where his family and in-laws were gathered and treated us as his own children.

That experience has never left my mind and when I graduated high school, I knew I couldn't leave youth ministry behind. I was at a different church by this time because of college but started helping with the middle school ministry. My freshman year didn't turn out the way I wanted and I came back to go to the university in the city in which I grew up. Chris asked if I would be interested in helping with the youth ministry I grew up in and I jumped at the opportunity. Fast forward to a few years later and at 24 years of age, I succeeded Chris Lynch as the youth pastor at Trinity United Methodist Church.

Can I tell you anything Chris Lynch ever taught me from a stage or on a retreat? Heck no. I have a hard time remembering what I eat for breakfast. I will never forget Chris' actions though. What he did for my sister and me was the most tangible expression of love I have ever experienced. He showed me Christ's love by what he did and I take that to heart every time I interact with our teens.

Patrick Griffey

Maxine Marshall (1917-2003)

Maxine Marshall was a Certified Christian Educator who started working an active volunteer in a large church in Omaha, then served as part-time and then full-time staff.

She and husband, Hal, and two daughters moved to Boulder, CO in the Rocky Mountain Conference. She became the first consecrated diaconal minister in the RMC in 1977. Her creativity knew no limits. She saw possibilities that others did not and she initiated and organized many new endeavors. She created the Media Resources Services ministry at the RMC Conference Center, which made it possible for Christian Educators and churches to borrow and use a variety of media resources. She served on several boards at the conference level and was on the Conference Board of Ministry for the RMC at the time of her retirement.

She served ten years as the Children's and Family Life Director at Mountainview United Methodist Church in Boulder and then created a model for congregational care that was used by numerous other congregations.

She served on two CEF Design Teams for CEF Conferences. She was chairperson for the one in Estes Park in October, 1992 and the one in Milwaukee, Wisconsin in 1990. As usual, the model included a number of new creative approaches. One of the joys of her later life was being asked to join a group of nationally-known Christian educators who met twice a year in various locations.

Maxine worked closely with Marlene Wilson who was a national leader in the Volunteer Management program in Boulder. Maxine was involved in Discipleship Resources for the General

Church. She created a flyer and booklet on "The Care and Feeding of Volunteers," which was a widely used resource for many years.

When many of us whom she had mentored were ordained as deacons in 1997, Maxine could not join us because she didn't have the academic requirements, but as always, she cheered all the rest of us on.

On a more personal note: I met Maxine in 1984 when I became a very part-time volunteer coordinator at St. Andrew United Methodist Church in Littleton, CO. Within months, I became the fulltime Christian Educator. The senior minister called me in to say that my first assignment was to immediately contact Maxine Marshall in Boulder to "learn the ropes." She was highly respected by every elder in the conference. Thus began a wonderful friendship with an incredible mentor. Maxine was always looking for new leadership in local churches and in the conference. She planted a seed of possibility and then nurtured and encouraged individuals in a thousand ways. She always encouraged attendance at training events. My first CEF Conference was in Savannah and I knew no one except Maxine.

There is no way to estimate how many of us Maxine mentored into ministry. We still find that she affected the lives of those we meet in various settings. She was energetic, enthusiastic, very perceptive, and she never accepted limitations or excuses. She urged me to run for the CEF Board of Directors. When I said that I was not known nationally, she said for me to let her handle that. I was elected and I served on the board from 1993 to 1997. It changed my life and my ministry.

She taught all of us to look at every church member to see the potential for leadership and then to plant that seed. Two of the persons I approached because of the potential I saw are now ordained deacons. Many others taught Sunday School, became active in social justice issues, and became committed to adult education. Maxine was always standing behind me in spirit as I encouraged others as she had encouraged me.

If I had to choose one lesson from her, it might be when she told me in every setting to learn to begin by asking questions rather than making statements. In the course of my professional ministry of twenty-five years, that advice stood me in good stead in many difficult and challenging situations.

Judy Davis, another retired ordained deacon in the Rocky Mountain Conference made this statement about Maxine: "She was such a part of so many of us. She always encouraged us on in ministry. I would not have done the things I did without her influence." Maxine was the best example of a leader that I have ever known. She changed many lives.

Marla Kauerz

CEF Mentors – David Melton (1953 –) and Mary Gene Lee

One definition of a mentor states that a mentor is a "more skilled or more experienced person, serving as a role model, teaches, sponsors, encourages, counsels, and befriends a less skilled or less experienced person for the purpose of promoting the latter's professional and/or personal development."[1] Less skilled and less experienced certainly described me when I showed up to my first Christian Education event. I had recently been assigned Christian Education responsibilities at the local church where I was serving as an Associate Pastor. I was excited for this transition as I had a passion for it, but I also knew I needed targeting training. This event would not only confirm my passion and give me guidance and also served as the beginning of lasting mentoring relationships. This event - Quest, as it was called - was also where I first heard of CEF (back then known as Christian Educators Fellowship) and met two persons who have served as wonderful mentors to me and to many others as well.

David Melton and I instantly jelled, due to both an interest in Atlanta Braves baseball and being one of the few guys who attended our local CEF chapter. David befriended me and also challenged me. David has been a role model of who a Christian Educator is and how to practice local church Christian Education ministry. David encouraged me and guided me regarding many local church issues along with my own professional development. Beyond even those, he has served as a friend and a colleague in ministry. I look forward to opportunities of reciprocating what David has modeled for me, especially as a male Christian educator.

The other person from Quest who has served as a valuable mentor for me is **Mary Gene Lee.** I first encountered Mary Gene when I went up before the Board of Ordained Ministry seeking Commissioning. More than a little nervous, I still remember being questioned by her about what material the tiny churches I served were using for children's faith formation. Luckily, I remembered "One-Room," for which she was a contributor (but I didn't know that at the time). What surprised me then but doesn't now that I know her, was her passion for formation that occurs at even the smallest of churches. She has not only counseled me with her wisdom but also inspired me with her passion that all are formed into the image of Christ.

Without mentors like David and Mary Gene Lee, I would not be nearly as experienced or possess the skills to match the God-given passion I have for faith formation. I am deeply indebted to both for their wisdom, guidance, and friendship.

Scott Hughes

Rev. Bobby Rackley

I have been influenced by many people in my life, however, there is one person in particular other than Jesus, who has influenced my life tremendously and continues to do so; his name is Bobby Rackley.

There is no one like Rev. Bobby Rackley. I first met Bobby when he came to serve as Youth Director at my home church, Christ Boulevard United Methodist Church, in Statesville, NC in 2005. Bobby came when our youth group needed him most. We were a rowdy bunch and needed someone to take charge, but at the same time would have fun with us and help us to grow in our relationships with Christ.

Bobby served as our paid part-time youth director but worked full-time as a high school English teacher. Bobby was not only my youth director but a friend. He always encouraged me and supported me during my high school years and even after I graduated and went to college. He knew how to bring the best out in everyone by his funny and dynamic personality.

Bobby saw more in me then I saw in myself. He continued to encourage me to apply for college even when I did not think it was for me. Bobby saw a call on my life that I did not see. He supported me and helped me to grow in my relationship with God. He would take me out for coffee or dinner and help me to discern my call into ministry.

Bobby served at Christ Boulevard for five years before he left to pursue a Master of Divinity degree at Duke University in Durham, NC. Bobby currently serves at Fuquay-Varina

United Methodist Church as Pastor of Christian Formation and Missional Outreach. He is currently working on a doctoral degree from Duke. From 2016-2017, I got to work alongside Bobby as I helped to lead a Youth Ministry program with him. What a privilege it was to work alongside someone who helped me in my faith formation; we got to work together in helping to lead other young people in their faith formation.

Bobby has a tremendous faith, and it motivates me to strengthen mine. I regard Bobby as one of my Christian mentors because of his strong devotion to the Lord. He has an extremely humorous, up-beat attitude about everything he does, which is a major motivator for me. I learned to smile even when I might have a bad day.

Edward Ramsey

Jim Sanderson

Jim Sanderson has always been a part of my ministry. Actually, I think I knew him as a teenager, before I was hired by First United Methodist Church in Webster Groves, but I don't remember if it was because of church camp at Epworth, or the secretary of the St. Louis South Sub-District UMYF, when he was Associate Council Director with Cannon Kinnard in the Conference Office in Clayton. Either way, by the time I found CEF in 1974, Jim was in Kirksville and so committed to CEF that he drove into St. Louis for every meeting.

Jim is the one who told me about good prices for construction paper at Bradburns (closed a couple of years ago); and asked me to do a program for CEF about my filing system. I remember he made a chair (maybe more?) out of cardboard and each year his family made a large ball out of Christmas cards. I remember he couldn't believe any pastor or Christian educator could take Monday off because that's when he got busy and organized his week. When I attended my first Annual Conference in 1980 (the year I was consecrated) he asked me to play the guitar for the celebration of the 200th anniversary of the Sunday School. That year, and every year until we moved to the CMC gym, Jim was in the back right corner of the sanctuary of Linn Memorial UMC with a cassette recorder taping the sessions for Archives & History. As a retiree, I've already missed three Annual Conference sessions, but I believe Jim's only missed this year.

I'm beginning to realize that my ministry history is inextricably intertwined with Jim's. A couple of times our CEF group took the trip to Cape Giarardeau after he was appointed there and discovered what a commitment it was on his part to be an active member of our group. After he retired they moved into the home they had built in Cape Girardeau. I regret never seeing the house that he and Martha designed. It sounded so practical and unique. They continued their ministry at Centenary UMC; but with senior citizens instead of teens.

If you haven't heard already, the reason Jim is on my mind is that he's in hospice due to advanced pancreatic cancer. The blessing is that he and Martha had moved a month or two ago to Chateau Girardeau, a senior living community, so they have the support they need. When I saw Jim last week he praised their children Todd and Diane for all they did to make the move complete.

Gary and I were blessed to be able to see Jim and say "good-bye" last week. He greeted me with, "I don't know how much time I have left." I replied with "none of us do." Jim's personality is still there as he replied with a smile, "but the view's shorter from here." At some point he said he'd see me in heaven. We'll have to have a CEF get-together when we all get to heaven -- and the trip won't be as long as Kirksville or Cape to St. Louis.

I thought that was all I would write; but memories continue to flood my mind. Jim shares my love of photography. I watched him take pictures when our group traveled for national conferences of CEF -- writing down each picture and the settings on his 35mm camera in a little notebook and stopping at each roadside historical marker. I was in the car with him when he drove Fritz & Etta Mae Mutti to the train station as we headed to the airport to fly home. I was not in the car with him and Laura Jo Smith and... in the early morning one year when they saw "horse statues" on the way to drop someone at the airport. The famous line was spoken on the way back, "the statues moved!" Can't remember at which national conference those events took place.

It meant a lot to 33-year-old me when Jim and Jo Ross and Laura Jo Smith arrived at Jefferson Barracks National Cemetery the morning we buried my father. I had not shown up at a weekend event that we had planned and they knew something major had happened if I had missed it. In the days before internet, I'm not sure how they figured out where and when to show up; but I was grateful they did.

Beth Anderson

Jane Shaffer (1947 -)

Rev. Jane Shaffer gave me my first real job in ministry. She accepted me for who I was with all of my doubts and skepticism; in fact, she actually encouraged me to wrestle with them. If I had to choose one word to describe her it would be accepting.

Jane took seriously her ordination vows to preach and teach the gospel. A native of Scotland, she served churches in Oregon. From the beginning of her ministry in 1971, she has always been a Christian educator, to this day, though she's now retired. She is still, and always will be a Christian educator. She was one of the founders of the Oregon-Idaho Conference CEF chapter in 1982.

Jane's work with children in worship is of particular note, and it has been a model for other Christian educators in the conference. This year three generations of the Shaffer-Lowery family women were members of the annual conference. Her daughter Eilidh followed her lead and is an elder in the Oregon-Idaho Conference of The United Methodist Church. Eilidh's husband is a Deacon in full connection.

Hospitality is a hallmark of her ministry as is her deep passion for God's people. She's not only accepting but creative, fun, and continues to serve in various ways in retirement.

Stacey Louellen

Nancy Spence (1936 -)

Nancy Spence was the director of Children's Ministry when I was a young child at Roswell United Methodist Church. While I don't remember much about the content, I do remember that Nancy was always there. Her reliable presence created a sense of safety and love that was critical to my early faith formation. I have known Nancy for more than 40 years.

Nancy helped my spiritual growth by inviting me to serve. She didn't send an all-call about the need for Sunday-School teachers. Rather, she pulled me aside and asked me to serve. I had no confidence in my ability to lead anyone in faith formation, but Nancy saw something in me, and that gave me the courage to try. My first experience, teaching 2 year olds, was simultaneously thrilling and terrifying. I discovered that I loved teaching, but I found a class full of toddlers overwhelming. Nancy was gracious and didn't offer any judgment or guilt when I asked for a year off. But Nancy is persistent and after my year off, she invited me again – this time she invited me to teach a 3rd grade class. Much better. I learned so much in preparing lessons: about the Bible, about myself, and about teaching. Nancy was supportive and created an environment where I could experience God at work through classroom interactions. She provided a creative framework, and trusted the process as well as God's timing in it.

Over the years Nancy and I served in various ministry settings together. I credit her with teaching me the thing I hold most dear about my approach to Christian Education: content is important, but relationships are everything. To be open to growth, we have to show up and be present – in our relationship with God and our relationships with others – and the best way to teach that is to model it.

Nancy is so good at the work because she gets to know people and connects them to meaningful service opportunities based on their unique gifts, talents, and desires – then she gets out of the way and lets them serve.

Lynne E Smith

Tanzy Tillet

Ms. Tanzy Tillet was a Sunday school teacher when I was about eight or nine years old and is a good friend of mine now. Previously she was my kindergarten teacher when I was about four. She tutored me when she was a preacher and was a great inspiration. A person of great determination, she encouraged me to not to just "go with the flow" and to sink my teeth into the Scriptures. Tanzy asked me to just look at scripture and think, "What is God trying to say through this?" She urged me to take scripture and actually use it, and to think deeply about it. She led me to consider what God might be calling me to do with my life. She was a constant source of encouragement all along the way and with lots of different things in life I owe a lot of my life and spiritual formation to my friend Tanzy.

Paul Wood

Marty Tobin

I have been in the church since I was born, and have heard about faith for 45 years. Since I was 17, I think that I've really put my "faith to action" in many ways. I'm truly thankful for that, and, in many ways, wish I would have been allowed to start sooner. My youth pastor, Marty Tobin, made sure that I had the opportunity to do mission work the very week that my bipolar mother allowed me. I truly became a Christian in 1986, and while in my youth group, I heard lessons week-in and week-out about how awesome Jesus is, and how great doing acts of mission would increase my faith. Sadly, my mother thought that she had to shelter me from everything. So my dad stepped in when I turned 17, and all the prayer, begging and convincing that Marty did finally pay off!

In 1993, my interest in youth ministry began while working at a boys' orphanage and volunteering at my high school youth ministry when I was a junior at Winthrop University. Marty strongly suggested that I attend a Bible college or seminary to finish my B.A., because he saw a future in Youth Ministry for me. I said, "Maybe later. My band is doing really well." In 1995, my father became so ill that he needed more managed care so I moved home. In January 1997, I transferred to the University of North Carolina in Charlotte (UNCC). By March that same year my degree path just did not feel right to me. I was working fulltime, taking care of parents, and trying to have a life so I took a break from college and fully intended on keeping my promise to my dad.

As I said, the "Wavy Train" band was rockin'! I played sax and did background vocals. Robert, Zach, Emmy, and Buford were my bandmates. Two struggled with drugs, and I drew a hard line against drugs. We opened for George Clinton, we headlined WestFest in Charlotte, we played nightclubs; man, it was ON! Shortly after those big events, it came down to a choice between their stopping drug use or my leaving the band. As I saw that they were not serious about seeking treatment or stopping their drug use, I quit the band in 1996, and promised my dad to finish my music/education degree, and keep full-time employment.

As I continued to care for my dad, I also dealt with my mother's bipolar illness, as she stayed un-medicated. I experienced lessons of humility and the rewards of that precious fruit that I may not have gotten, and am SO thankful to God, as those lessons have sustained me! Even though I was no longer a teenager, Marty was there for me -- through my dad's job loss, illness, my mother's condition -- Marty Tobin picked up the phone when I called, and prayed with me and for me! Praise God! He is the reason that I entered into youth ministry in 2005.

Last year Marty had a heart attack. I arrived at the waiting room, reunited with his family and youth group friends, and over the course of that day, about 200 people came to see him. He's fine now, still preaching and teaching, and playing with his grandkids. Marty's slogan to all of us was to "be real" and that's what I try to instill in the teens in my youth group. I hope to be that quality of person and pastor.

Bradley Keith

Don Webb, Robert Browning, and Chuck Foster

Dr. Don Webb was the pastor of our church when I was in high school. He taught me that faith wasn't just in the Bible, that it was real and his faith was dynamic. He went to Mississippi and marched in the civil rights movement. Don took me to hear Dr. Martin Luther King, Jr. preach when I was just a sophomore in high school so that I could get a sense of what the church could be.

Then in my seminary education I had the great joy of having two professors, **Dr. Robert Browning** and **Dr. Chuck Foster**, who continued to push me to think about education in the church in tremendously different ways. Ultimately they led me to become a professor of Christian education until the new role [at Martin Methodist College]. Chuck served as a mentor to me at times when I needed a sounding board.

Among the qualities that these three shared was that you could see in all three of them a dynamic faith and acceptance of where you were in your faith but they always challenged you to move forward. They opened up scripture and tradition to see that they actually could deal with problems in culture at the time.

Ed Trimmer

Myra Hogan

Myra was friends with my parents before they got married. One day Mom asked if I knew Myra, and I said, "Yes, I have a [CEF] meeting with her every month." I learned so much from her because she was willing to help me out when I was first hired. Our monthly meetings sometimes would turn into complaint sessions or we just shared ideas about what was going on in our work lives. Myra taught a lot about confidentiality. She was one of the core people that kept the CEF group in San Diego going for a long time.

Myra always wanted to continue education, hers, and for children's and adult ministries. She always got incredible teachers and professors to come in and speak to adult classes. She's a good role model and friend.

Dee Berra

IV.
Professors and Teachers

Susan Carmichael (1923 -)

During my formative years prior to college, I did not have a single female role model who served professionally in ministry. I was raised in a very loving and grace filled Southern Baptist Church (that is now a very influential CBF congregation) where women exhibited passionate and missional leadership as laity. We did have one female Minister of Music/Youth who was exceptional but was a musician by profession. As I reflect back on this important piece of my faith journey, I am not sure how I arrived at Pfeiffer College in 1975 committed to serve the church as a Christian Educator and yet I knew that was the path that God intended for me to follow. God had Susan Carmichael ready to model for me and to guide and advise me in a way that shaped the past 40 years of my life.

Throughout my entire educational journey at Pfeiffer, Professor Susan Carmichael committed her heart and soul to preparing students to become servant leaders and to transform the world. Education and the church seemed to be her entire life! She lived in faculty housing on campus and we often saw her working in her yard (she loved to garden) and she seemed to always be available to listen and give advice. Susan was tough on us and expected the best. She encouraged us to engage others in ministry, "to work ourselves out of a job" by equipping others to be in ministry with us and not just doing ministry for others.

At the time, I didn't think she liked me as much as other students because I was Baptist, but upon reflection I realize now that she knew I had the capacity to be a strong voice for young people and for others striving to follow in a path of discipleship. She challenged me to find my voice and to be confident and passionate in every aspect of ministry. Imagine my surprise to learn that when I applied to serve a United Methodist congregation, it was Susan's glowing recommendation that helped me get that job.

I joined CEF in the fall of 1981 under the encouragement of Rev. Melvin McIntosh and it became the center of my professional community both in the conference and nationally. I took great pride in attending national and regional CEF events and introducing myself as "one of Susan's girls" as everyone who is anyone in CEF knew exactly what that meant! I was hardly the only one. She taught me to not take "no" as a final answer but to find ways to achieve a goal or to empower a ministry beyond all odds and expectations.

In 1997, I accepted the mantle of Susan Carmichael when I returned to my alma mater to serve as the first full time director of the Masters program at Pfeiffer University. For the past 21 years, I have channeled her tenacity and perseverance to forge new paths in theological education for those gifted and called to the educational and other areas of specialized ministries.

It is still truly a joy to visit Miss Carmichael at Brooks Howell Home in Asheville. She "holds court" at lunchtime where she is surrounded by dedicated and committed servants of the church as they continue to be in ministry together. If she is not in the dining room, you may find her working in the library! Yes, at 95+ she is still working and sharing her gifts as much as possible as she did as a faculty member at Pfeiffer for 35 years. When I visit with her, she is still the teacher, asking me about my work, about Pfeiffer and our commitment to the church. I will be forever grateful to Miss Susan Carmichael, a true servant of Jesus Christ and his church.

Kathleen Kilbourne

Susan Carmichael (1923 -) and Carrie Goddard (1912-1999)

Susan Carmichael was my professor at Pfeiffer College in the 1970's and she started me on the path that I am on now. I have kept up with her for forty years now. One of the things she did for me was to point me in the direction of Scarritt College to connect with another professor there, **Carrie Goddard,** who became my professor for two years. She just opened up for me an entire world of caring for children. She taught me how to do ministry with children. My ministry has always been about, for and with children. She had a love for children that you could not help but feel and know that she cared.

They were both gentle, patient, and great storytellers. They both just loved children and that showed in everything that they did.

Daphne Flegal

Margaret Ann Crain (1943 -)

I will forever be grateful for the opportunity to serve with Margaret Ann Crain at Peachtree United Methodist Church in Atlanta. Margaret Ann provided an environment where those committed to Christian Education could learn, practice and grow. It was an invaluable, experiential, and creative way of being in ministry. She is a wise woman who has mentored many Christian educators and Deacons throughout her career whether serving in the local church or on the faculty of Garrett-Evangelical Theological Seminary. My ministry and life have been blessed by her teaching and friendship.

Margaret Ann's service to the Church is deep and wide. Her books, including those that she's written with her husband, Jack Seymour, are required reading for serious seminary and theology students, but are easily accessible to laity and clergy alike. With the encouragement and support of Dr. Linda Vogel and President Fisher, Margaret Ann started and was the Director of Deacon Education at Garrett-Evangelical

 Theological Seminary. Supposedly retired now, she is working on another book, this one about United Methodist Women bishops. She has served The United Methodist Church in many capacities over the years, from the local church where we served to General Conference. Additionally, she's written many articles and monographs. Her

passion for the ministry of the deacon and for social justice are well known.

When not working for the Church one way or another, Professor Emeritus Margaret Ann Crain spends time with grandchildren and her quilts, which are exquisite.

Debby Fox

Dr. Mary Alice Douty Edwards
(1913-2014)

Mary Alice was my teacher and faculty advisor while I pursued my master's degree in Religious Education at Wesley Theological Seminary in Washington DC, 1979-1981. She served on Wesley's faculty from 1957-1983. She was a creative teacher who emphasized the importance of life-long learning, which I took to heart in my ministry. As a youth minister, I began in 1990 visiting college students on their campuses, intent on maintaining their connection to the church past high school, convinced that choices about religious identity and practice really take place in young adulthood. In 25 years, I visited students at their schools in 22 states and DC from Harvard and MIT to the University of the Pacific. I have known her for 30 years.

As a pioneer who was not encouraged in a profession, she challenged me to be professional, to be serious about my calling, and be focused on my own life-long learning. She convinced me of the value of collegial support groups, especially CEF.

One day Dr. Mary Alice Edwards announced to her Christian Education degree candidates that she had paid for membership in Christian Educators Fellowship (CEF) for all of us, and that we constituted our own seminary chapter. That got me started. Dr. Edwards led us to be involved in the regional CEF conference held in Washington DC in 1980.

Dr. Edwards had long experience in Christian education at the local church and conference level prior to her seminary career. What made her great was that she was innovative and cared deeply for her students, and I am one of those grateful persons whom she helped in faith formation and professional development.

Wesley Seminary President McAllister-Wilson remembers Edwards as a person of strength and determination – and as an avid sailor. "She was, indeed, the captain of her own boat," he said. "Some years ago, as she started to go blind, she undertook to memorize the whole United Methodist Hymnal so that she could continue to sing along confidently. To paraphrase that great ending of the poem 'Invictus,' she was the master of her fate, the captain of her soul." Her legacy lives on today.

Author unknown

Dr. Patty Meyers (1952 -)

I first met Dr. Patty as a graduate student at Pfeiffer University in 2013. Before I even stepped foot into my first class with her, I had been told by many: "You will love her!" Walking into the first session of *Spiritual Formation* I was met by seemingly chaotic activity by an extraordinary number of graduate students in one room. For a while there the craziness in the room seemed overwhelming; but Dr. Patty Meyers turned out to be a rare gem and one of the blessings in my life that I will never stop thanking God for…ever. Her faith and her ethics are illustrated in what she teaches, how she teaches it and how she lives her life. Her style is one of constant encouragement and challenge. She invests so much of herself into her students and the many that she mentors and directs spiritually.

"Everything Teaches" and *"Blessed are the flexible, they bend and don't break"* are two phrases that I use as a compass in my coming and going. Fellow students and colleagues agree that her *everything teaches* philosophy is solidified in the way she is always early, ready and set up with curriculum, materials, games, and any and all other resources she thinks we might be interested in or could find useful. Likewise *being flexible* has made it a lot easier to work with those that are a little [maybe even more than a little] less flexible. It has created awareness in me to be deliberate about what I teach verbally and non-verbally.

I have learned that Christian education and faith formation are more than just science and theology. I have learned to live *everything matters* and *every person is worth fighting for*. A most powerful impact on me, and now my children too, is

Dr. Patty's insistence on people with disabilities/ learning developmental issues being referred to as "differently abled" and not "disabled."

Dr. Patty lives her beliefs in social justice issues out in real life. I will never forget how devastated she was over the death of so many people in a Bangladesh clothing factory fire. She went through her closet and threw out anything made in Bangladesh. What an inspiration!

I will always be grateful to Dr. Patty for her insistence that we develop for ourselves healthy spiritual disciplines. When I experienced extreme stress within my workplace, Dr. Meyers met with me and guided me on a deeply spiritual level to a place where I could see things in perspective and remain quiet to listen to what God wanted from me. Her experience is so vast and she is willing to share both victories and setbacks. Was it not for her, my life would have been significantly harder and my faith would have been static; instead she has inspired and empowered me to be so much more than I thought I could be.

I attended my first CEF Conference in 2014 at her invitation. She made sure to introduce me to as many people as possible. She speaks highly of all her colleagues and encourages me constantly to read and read and read. Her book recommendations are gems and my bookshelves are full! She is generous about sharing the "secrets of the trade." Dr. Meyers is constantly recommending websites, institutions and other resources that could be useful. She calls these 'gifts.' Under her tutelage I have been able to implement many changes and improvements in my life and ministry almost immediately. She lights flames in hearts of persons who want to educate the world in Christ and for Christ. Dr. Meyers is passionate about equipping all Christian educators so that we may stand up and stand together to ensure that faith formation bring about a positive change in Christian Education that has true, long lasting and life-changing results in the world in which we live .

Dr. Patty Meyers is by far and away the one person who I would point to as my most influential faith former. She taught me not only how to organize the way to do Christian education but to authentically live my faith in all I do. I took a lot of classes from her at Pfeiffer University. I have been blessed to receive my Christian education training and education from such a wonderful and insanely knowledgeable woman of Christ. Dr. Meyers has inspired me to extend myself more. I too want to be able to share of myself so that others may grow and go on and become the best possible Faith Formation leaders. She is a very focused, dedicated, creative and gifted Christian educator because she loves what she teaches. Wherever my life and my calling lead me, I will share Dr. Patty's wisdom and talk about her and try to teach, lead and inspire like her.

I am truly thankful that I can call Dr. Patty Meyers, a faithful Kingdom recruiter, beloved daughter of Christ and Christian Educator par excellence, *my friend*.

Charmaigne Van Rooyen

Patty Meyers (1952 -)

Dr. Patty Meyers is by far and away the one person who I would point to as my most influential faith former. She taught me not only how to organize the way to do Christian education but to authentically live my faith in all I do. I took a lot of classes from her at Pfeiffer University. She helped with the nuts and bolts but also reminded me continually that we are to be within God's will when we live our lives. She reminds me to not forget that it is okay to ask Him what it is we're supposed to be doing. Dr. Meyers reminds me to pray a lot. She not only talks the talk but walks the walk. She has an amazing spirit about her and you can tell that she is filled with the Holy Spirit.

Debby Stykes

Dr. Richard (Dick) Murray
(1924 - 2002)

Dr. Dick Murray was one of my seminary professors at Perkins School of Theology at Southern Methodist University in Dallas, Texas. He taught there for 28 years. It seemed that everything he said was golden. If you knew him, you would just be easily inspired by him. He had a dry wit and was unconventional in his approach to most things. He loved teaching. He loved working with youth.

Dick Murray was a colorful character who could often be seen wearing his *Des Colores* suspenders, cowboy boots and bolero tie (if he wore a tie). His book, *Teaching the Bible to Adults and Youth* was a classic and it was revised and re-published. He was passionate about Christian education in general and biblical literacy in particular. Probably his most lasting legacy will be the pedagogical methods he provided for *Disciple Bible Study,* which came out in 1993 and continues to evolve into new forms today.

He was a long time member and supporter of CEF and UMASCE (United Methodist Association of Scholars of Christian Education). He was a major reason why I got involved in CEF thirty or forty years ago, as well as for the fellowship of being with other Christian educators. If I had to sum up his qualities in a word or two, I would say awesome and great. He was truly a great teacher and friend.

Gary Linehardt

Dick Murray (1924 - 2002)

My very first CEF conference was in Savannah in1984, and that's when I met Dick Murray. He literally changed her life. The man was so incredible. He knew about how people learned and he knew how to teach/learn. He was truly a legend in his own time and he turned everything around for me. He changed the way I teach and how I bring people into the ministry. The man was absolutely incredible. A hallmark of his teaching was humor and he instinctively – intuitively – knew how people learn, and he used that to his advantage. That was the beginning. He could read people. I learned more from him than I did in my undergraduate teaching degree. He was a wonderful, wonderful man and is truly missed. Dick was an amazing man.

Barbara Bruce

Jack Lee Seymour (1948 -)

In 1983 I took a summer course at Scarritt Graduate School in Nashville called *Teaching the Bible*. I was a green Christian educator hired by the congregation where my family attended, temporarily and part time, "until they could get someone from the seminary." My new friends at the Missouri East Conference CEF had encouraged me to pursue professional certification so I travelled to Nashville to take courses in the summer. The young man teaching that course was Dr. Jack Seymour. He inspired me to take Bible study seriously and to share my learning with the congregation where I served. That commitment remains with me to this day and guides most of my teaching scholarship.

Jack Seymour was raised in Kokomo, Indiana and was very active in the neighborhood United Methodist Church so it is no surprise that he eventually attended Vanderbilt Divinity School where he received the M.Div. and D. Min. degrees. He was fascinated with history which led him to complete a PhD in history at George Peabody College of Vanderbilt. His earliest faculty positions were in field education, but he came to Scarritt to teach religious education and that has remained his primary identity as scholar and teacher.

From the beginning, Jack was a supporter and attendee at CEF conferences. Countless graduates of Scarritt and Garrett-Evangelical Theological Seminary took courses with Jack and were inspired about teaching in the church. Countless others read his books on religious education or participated in workshops he led at CEF and have sought to reflect his values of taking the Bible seriously, attending to the learning styles of people in his classes, and offering opportunities for reflection and transformation in the midst of learning.

Christian faith for Jack is always about doing the works of justice and following Jesus. Thus, he advocates for universal health care, inclusion of all, caring for the marginalized, welcoming the stranger, feeding the widow and orphan, and loving your neighbor. In his own words, he seeks "to empower the church to teach and live `the way of Jesus;' to describe approaches to interfaith religious education; and to empower the people of God to become interpreters of scripture." His interests in retirement continue to be helping the Church to live and teach the "way of Jesus." His recent book, *Teaching Biblical Faith: Leading Small Group Bible Studies* is a wonderful, succinct compendium of his commitments and his scholarship!

In the interest of full disclosure, Jack and I were married in 1998 and we have worked together on several books including *A Deacon's Heart* which has helped many to explore a call to ordination and the order of deacon.

Margaret Ann Crain

Vickie Sigmon

I have been blessed to have a few amazing people that have been influential to my faith formation. Vickie Sigmon from Open Arms is one of those people. During my undergraduate degree I needed to have an internship, to have practical experience.

Dana McKim, who was in charge of assigning internships at the university, told me that he wasn't going to put me in a church setting, which surprised me because that was my goal at the time. He told me little about this non-profit in my home city of Winston-Salem that I was going to be working for that summer and told me to go meet the Church and Community Worker that was over it.

So, I went home for the summer and drove up to this white, two-story, historical looking house in a pretty sketchy part of town. It had a white fence and a big sign on the top of the porch roof that said Open Arms Community. I went in the front door and saw this lady, who had crazy red hair and looked half-crazed herself. My first thought was, "Oh Lord, Dana, where did you send me?", but I introduced myself to her and met for a bit. She told me that this non-profit was through The United Methodist Church and it helps the low-resource local families, which happen to be a 100% Hispanic population. She told me the different events they do throughout the week for the kids and families, and then told me when to come in. I was a bit hesitant, but I figured Dana knew what he was doing, and so within a week or so I went.

Open Arms has quite a schedule. Mondays were Girl Scouts, Tuesdays were tutoring during the school year, Wednesdays were Bible Study for the adults and childcare for the kids, and Thursdays were music nights for kids. She took me to different parts of town I never knew about, to families living in section 8 housing, and introduced me to all sorts of people. Her love and passion for the marginalized populations set a fire in my heart.

While working under her guidance, I learned that I have gifts for children and for the ministry of presence. Her ideals challenged my own and I learned so much about myself for the short three months I was there. I created friendships with people I would have never done on my own. I learned about the issues the families dealt with that we served. I grew close to multiple families and I had found a second home at Open Arms. Dana came during my time there to do a site evaluation and his words will stay with me, "I have never seen you this calm." It made me realize, that like Vickie, my heart was a missional one. My heart was broken for the marginalized people. My heart was for the least, the last, and the lost. My heart was set on fire for social justice. What I thought my calling was changed during my time at Open Arms, and I will forever be grateful for Vickie, the families, and my time there.

Brandy Saltzman

Nelle G. Slater (1928-2016)

Born in Pecos TX, she moved to Glendale, CA at the age of four. Nelle was not raised in the church but she responded to her call to ministry at age 15 at an MYF (Methodist Youth Fellowship) camp and became a lifelong United Methodist.

She attended Whittier College, later attaining the M.RE and Ph.D. at Boston University. She was influenced by Professor Robert Ulrich (Harvard), and quoted him: "To constantly create and recreate the saving sense of the sacredness of life within a freedom loving society, this is the noblest and most necessary task of Religious Education."

She taught at Whittier for a few years, and spent nearly 20 years at Christian Theological Seminary in Indiana as Professor of Christian Education. She was the founder and director of the Center for Congregational Education. With a Lilly grant, she led another of the center's most important projects, a National Faculty Seminar in 1982-1987.

She was active in REA (Religious Education Association) and APRRE (the Association of Professors and Researchers in Religious Education) as well as CEF (Christian Educators Fellowship). She was a consummate organizer. She used her organizing skills when served as President of the United Association of Scholars of Christian Education (UMASCE). With Janet Fishburn, Mary Elizabeth Moore, Linda J. Vogel and Elizabeth Box Price, they wrote *People of a Compassionate God*, published in 2003 by UMASCE.

She did less writing than other academic colleagues, but her legacy is us. She was committed to women, global and interfaith issues. Debora Junker, Sandy Eisenberg Sasso, Linda Vogel and I were grateful recipients of her mentoring for personal and professional development. I learned a lot from her. She was a no-nonsense woman. Nelle didn't mince words; she said what needed to be said and the wise listened to her.

She was a teacher, administrator in graduate and undergraduate institutions and a role model. This quote from Nelle summarizes her passion: "The inadequacies of institutional tradition and practices need to be examined with dialogue with the One who still stands at the door and knocks. Religious Education calls forth the aliveness that is food for the meals with the invited Guest."

Nelle retired to Redding, CA to be with family. From there she did consultations and visits, organized adult education and kept teaching at the local United Methodist Church. She was a strong, courageous pioneering Christian educator who modelled the way and helped form the faith for many.

Patty Meyers

Rosemary Smith

Rosemary Smith was the preschool director in our local Presbyterian church where her father was senior pastor. When my children were very young, she invited me to participate in the church while also being a preschool mom. That invitation turned out to be life-changing. Her influence and our daughters' love for that preschool found me quitting my regular teaching job to teach in the preschool and work for Rosemary. She was an amazing person who made natural connections between faith and all of life. She helped parents and kids make those connections, too. With her guidance, I became a much better parent and a much better teacher, which had a strong influence on the faith formation of my children and me.

Debby Fox

My Students

It's a well-known fact that teachers learn more than their students. You know "your stuff" if you can make it come alive so that others can learn. Truthfully, no one can make anyone learn anything, even if coerced; at some level free will kicks in and the desire to learn comes out one way or another.

I am a lifelong learner and I've been a Christian educator all my adult life. I first taught Vacation Bible School at age 14, then many Sunday school classes and after school programs for children. Even as a public school teacher my identity was Christian educator. Since then, I have taught college, university and seminary students for the past 31 years in addition to Mission U, many workshops, pastors schools, camps and retreats.

For most of my 31 years in higher education, I have annually taught courses in faith development and spiritual formation. I've led pilgrimages to Iona and taught time-honored spiritual practices to people of all ages and stages of life in order to assist persons to grow in their relationships with the Divine.

A long time ago I learned from Parker Palmer that we teach who we are. I couldn't stand in from of a class every semester and fake my own faith. Students questioned and challenged me to authentically live my faith with them even as I sought to serve God and them. I have had wonderful students who played profound parts in my faith formation. They've kept me honest and humble, up to date in my discipline, and in constant prayer.

It has been a holy privilege to walk alongside students for whatever amount of time we have. I've learned so much from them and I am deeply grateful. To all my students, I ask forgiveness for my faults and foibles, and I say thank you for letting me walk a few steps on your faith journeys.

Patty Meyers

Dr. Theodore Tremble

In 1995 after I finished my B.A. in Chemistry in Los Angeles, I moved back to North Carolina, the place of my birth. I had taken science classes with Dr. Tremble at Gaston College before moving to California to finish my degree. I went back to visit and help Dr. Tremble in the lab and tutor students. I decided to take the course "Differential Equations" at Gaston College so that I would be an official student there.

I was working part-time in Dallas, N.C. for a company that performed waste water management for the city. Dr. Tremble retired from his professorship at Gaston College, and as a high school teacher at Gaston Day School. He was moving to Banner Elk to work as a part-time Assistant Professor at Lees-McRae College. He needed help moving his 1,500 books there. I learned that he had been a missionary in Taiwan, in the late 1950s. Now his goal was to eventually start a school in Guatemala, providing education for the people there. I also discovered that Dr. Theodore Tremble not only held a doctorate in chemistry but had a master's degree in theology. He was very devoted to the Presbyterian Church.

I decided to quit my job in quality control and move to Banner Elk, helping him move his books and start a greenhouse at the college. As I got to know Dr. Tremble better, I noticed that he was a deeply religious man who sacrificed many of the luxuries of life, devoting his time as an educator and mentor to others, including me.

Dr. Tremble had some rare books. He let me read a book by Pierre Teilhard de Chardin, (1881 – 1955) a Jesuit priest, translated in English from the original French language. The book was hard for me to understand at the time, but it emphasized the unity and communication of people from all over the world. He predicted that people from every corner of the earth would begin to communicate with each other, and begin to understand and learn from each other. The author seemed to have a deep compassion for acceptance of others, and an openness for different viewpoints in a loving a gentle way, free of judgment and gossip. Dr. Tremble was a very loving person with whom I could talk and know that he understood me. He really listened to what I said and how I felt. He was extremely dedicated to the advancement of humankind in education and science. He would not tolerate gossip, and he never spoke badly about anyone. He always had positive words to say about others, focusing on their strengths not weaknesses.

The dedication that Dr. Tremble demonstrated, his love for humanity, growth, and achievements, was a strong inspiration in my life. He gave me faith in the goodness of humanity that comes from God. He was a real person who wanted to do the real work of God, and that is what he did. I will always cherish the time that I had with him. He expressed to me that he was losing his short-term memory but could remember things in his distant past very clearly. Even under this difficult circumstance of his old age, he still was a light on my path, giving me faith in God through the good works of humanity and their compassion for others.

Timothy Farris

Linda Jane Vogel (1940 - 2017)

I used to say that I wanted to be Linda Vogel when I grew up. As I write this essay I am aware that she influenced countless students at Westmar College and Garrett-Evangelical Theological Seminary, as well as many Sunday School students, parishioners, workshop participants, and more. When the deadline for contributions to this book came and went without an entry about Linda, I had to include her. She was a consummate Christian educator, longtime CEF member and served on the board (including as president), a Deacon in The United Methodist Church, and active member of several professional groups.

The author of books and many articles, she co-authored a couple books with her husband of 58 years, the Rev. Dr. Dwight Vogel. In every role of life Linda shared hospitality, kindness, and worked for justice. "Even as she was dying last fall, she went to her church to be on a panel about inclusion for lgbtq folks and shared her story of how her heart was opened by her relationship with a gay person who opened her life and struggles to Linda," remembers Margaret Ann Crain. She looked after people in a very low-key way that was so endearing. She embodied true discipleship.

Linda was very instrumental in Garrett-Evangelical's development of Deacon Education. She convinced President Fisher that Margaret Ann could head up the deacon studies program. She never shied away from advocating for anything she believed was important and hundreds, if not thousands, of people are better for her efforts.

I met Linda and Dwight when I first began attending Calvary United Methodist Church in Le Mars, Iowa. It wasn't too long before I became a United Methodist, a Sunday school teacher and a singer in the church choir. Linda was the Director of Christian education and Dwight was the choir director, in addition to their service on the faculty of Westmar College. Eventually Calvary Church sent me off to Garrett-Evangelical Theological Seminary. I truly admired both of them: their commitment to each other, to Christ and the Church, to their three children, to Christian Education in general and CEF in particular, to the Order of St. Luke, peace and justice. I always stayed in contact with them through the years; they have been lifelong friends and are among the most important people in my life and helped become the person I am today. Thanks be to God for Linda J. Vogel and Dwight.

Patty Meyers

V.
Authors

Delia Halverson

I have known Delia Halverson for 26 years. Delia was instrumental in building my intent to lead others in their faith development. She led by example and shared her own faith with the young children at our church. Though she volunteered in our congregation (was not a paid staff person), her work was a big part of its ministry.

Delia was passionate about Christian education. She was innovative and creative and seemed to truly love the young children of our church. She helped me to see how truly easy it was to connect and helped me learn to guide my own children in developing their faith. As a young mother, her influence helped me see the connection between faith and home.

Delia is a Christian educator, writer, workshop leader, mentor, friend, and much more. She has written approximately 30 books, dozens of articles, and is generous with her wisdom and time. She is a long-time member of CEF. I am grateful for her and to her.

Juanita Tatum

Kenneth E. Hagin, Sr. (1917-2003) and Juanita Thomas

My clearest recollection of a person or persons who were most influential in my faith formation is a book written by Kenneth E. Hagin, Sr., that I encountered stationed at a Naval Base in southern Georgia in the late 1980's. I later gave that same book to my eldest sister (whom I believe was unsaved at the time). Rev. **Juanita Thomas** has been ministering in Washington, DC for nearly two decades. This book was a teaching on being led by the Holy Spirit and it played an integral part in my life as well my sister's.

Kenneth Erwin Hagin was an American preacher born in McKinney, Texas, the son of Lillie Viola Drake Hagin and Jess Hagin. According to Hagin's own testimony, he was born with a deformed heart and not expected to live. After his conversion to Christianity in 1933, he is said to have died three times in 10 minutes due to his deformed heart. He recovered and went on to live a devout life for God that included preaching, teaching, and writing books like the one that contributed immensely to my spiritual and faith formation.

I recently reviewed one of Kenneth Hagin's sermons online in which he spoke about the Holy Spirit living on the inside of every born-again Christian – being an "inward witness" - giving the "green light" to move forward with an idea or project, or on the other hand, giving one the conviction to wait on God. He reminded Christians to learn to listen to that "inward witness" because that Spirit of God will bear witness; and thus, lead believers into all truth (John 16:13). I found it encouraging to hear him preach that, "The spirit of man is the candle of the Lord" (Proverbs 20:21).

That single book, alongside the Bible, and its teachings made the Holy Spirit very real to me. During the time that my sister was visiting me in Georgia, she noticed a change in me, which led to mentioning of this very impactful book entitled *How You Can Be Led by the Spirit of God* (1978). I gave my sister that book, and she recalls now that she read it on the train ride back to Maryland. I cannot attest to the real impact that the book had on my sister's life, but she became an ordained minister about a decade later.

My sister has played an important role in my faith formation since that time. She has been a constant prayer partner, community leader in the Church, and teaching minister, as well as, a great influence on my spiritual life and commitment to the Lord. I can say without hesitation that she loves the Lord dearly and has been a true beacon of hope for me and other immediate and blended family members. She is always there in the time of need, and she keeps the prayer line always open.

Michael Thomas

VI.
Village

"It takes a Village"

In considering the challenge to write about someone who had an impact on my life as a Christian and as a Christian Educator, I began to think of many people. I think of course of **my parents** and of the **many dedicated lay teachers in our church, East Highland Methodist Church in Columbus, GA,** who came every Sunday with a prepared lesson for our Sunday school class, such as **my third grade teacher Mrs. Hogan**. I remember the children's Sunday school room where we met and the poster on the wall with the verse, "I was glad when they said unto me, Let us go into the house of the Lord." (Psalm 122:1 KJV)

I remember the wonderful leaders of our Vacation Bible School each year, both adults and youth, and looked up to them with the anticipation of helping with VBS when I became a teen. I remember our pastor and the genuine, dedicated laity who guided us in our youth classes and MYF group, such as **Ruth Culpepper** who became a "living legend" among the youth for her love, dedication and wisdom she so freely offered for so many years. We were encouraged to develop and use our leadership skills and to grow through planning and leading programs, events, and worship. My faith was nurtured and deepened and I discovered an excitement in using my gifts in these ways.

I found role models in the college and seminary students who worked as part time Youth Directors with our youth group as part of their preparation for becoming pastors and I began to consider if that was something I might like to do. (So "thank you" to **Rev. Ronnie and Julia Culpepper, Rev. Dick Reese, and Rev. Joel Dent**.) I also vividly remember a conversation with **Margaret Greer**, a close friend who attended a nearby Methodist church. We were just 15 years old in 1962 and were thinking about our future. She talked about the possibility of becoming a Director of Christian Education. Seeds were planted and somehow that thought emerged again in my senior year of college, when I felt God leading me to enter Duke Divinity School to prepare to become a Director of Christian Education. At Duke I was blessed by the leadership of outstanding faculty, especially **Dr. James "Mickey" Efird** who inspired my love of Bible study. I remember becoming so excited about the book of Acts that I was opening conversations with people in the cafeteria line with the question, "Have you read the book of Acts?!"

I have a special memory of **Jean Bowman**, who was the first full-time Director of Christian Education serving in a church that I had the opportunity to meet. I remember visiting this role model in her church office when I was a seminary student. Then as a young DCE, it was very encouraging to see her at national CEF conferences and have the chance to visit.

When I arrived in Jackson, MS, in 1973 to become the first full-time DCE at Christ United Methodist Church, a thriving young church bursting with opportunity, I was surrounded by genuine and talented lay Christian leaders in children's ministry and youth ministry, including **Julia Bishop and Donna Slater** from whom I learned a great deal about excellence in early childhood education. Together we worked to start the CUMC Weekday Preschool, a vital part of the church's children's ministry.

I was also welcomed by a very active MS Conference Christian Educators Fellowship. This group provided a wonderful place of professional and spiritual growth and warm fellowship during my 13 years in the MS Conference, with Christian Education legends such as **Jimmy and Joy Carr, Jill Beshell, Jimmy and Delia Dabbs, and Florence Jo Corban.** One memorable and impactful adventure together was attending the National Christian Educators Fellowship Conference in Philadelphia, PA, in 1976, where we joined with many other old and new friends from across the country. The relationships developed at CEF events provided encouragement and nurtured joy and enthusiasm within me that helped sustain my ministry.

National CEF conferences through the years (beginning with Boston in 1972) have always been extremely meaningful in shaping my life and ministry. This brings me to name a "top notch" legend, **R. Harold Hipps** and to give thanks for his leadership. R's creativity, skill and joyful spirit permeated the CEF conferences that he helped to plan. I learned so much from the many learning experiences offered, including opportunities to study with legendary Christian Education leaders and professors such as **Donald Griggs**, a major role model for creative approaches to teaching and teacher training. Through participation in these conferences I also learned great ways to organize events. Most importantly, I learned ways to unleash my own creativity as well as the gifts of those with whom I served in my role as a Christian Educator throughout my 40+ years of ministry.

Jean Foster

The People of Pine Grove United Methodist Church

A stone's throw from the Carolinas state line on Highway 18 in Cleveland County there is a white wooden sign. The sign reads, "Pine Grove United Methodist Church, Founded 1830." The small red brick church sits on a dirt road. This small congregation in the woods of Cleveland County shaped much of the person I am today.

With most of the pastors being retired elders, the ministry of the church is primarily lay driven. For example, when I was younger, the church did not have a children's Sunday school class, but as the number of children increased, lay people volunteered to rotate regularly to teach. Most of the events at the church were "whole church" events, with the forty or so members all working together to put on Egg hunts, Luaus, and Halloween parties.

My most significant memories come from Wednesday night youth group meetings. For small rural churches like ours, youth group encompassed any children who wanted to come. In the late 1980s, my cousin, Wendy, started college in teacher education. The church gave her a small amount of money to buy supplies and she became the volunteer leader. We either met in the small children's classroom off the sanctuary or on the front steps of the church. Our numbers ranged from 6-12 kids of all ages. She taught using a variety of approaches, including art, nature exploration, songs, and storytelling. I remember learning the books of the Bible one summer with songs, flash cards, and games.

My mother, "Mama," was always there in support of my cousin. I remember as my siblings and I reached school age she became more involved with the lessons and activities. One summer in the early nineties, Pine Grove decided to begin having a Vacation Bible School. Mama organized it for the first several years. I remember her leading the assemblies. We said pledges to the American flag, Christian flag, and the Bible. We sang songs, heard stories, and went to our small groups. One year, the theme was "2000 Ark Avenue." During "Hip-Hip-Hip-Hippopotamus," a song about God's love, Mama and several other leaders danced around the sanctuary with a giant pink stuffed hippo. Another year, she had a stuffed animal puppet named Sparkplug who led the music with us.

As we got older, Mama and the other leaders encouraged us to begin leading lessons and helping plan events. I remember each child leading a lesson on a different book of the Bible. I made a Jeopardy game for one lesson. Another person had us use playdough. Another had us paint. We began to help design activities for the younger children at parties, Vacation Bible School, and mission projects.

Through the efforts of my parents, my cousin, and people I know and love, I grew in my faith and abilities. Their resourcefulness, willingness to try new things, and a faith that lead them to nurture and care for those in their community formed my understanding of God and lead me into my vocation. I rarely get back to Pine Grove for worship, but I hold these memories in my heart, as I watch the friends and family there continue to nurture the children of the church.

Jonathan LeMaster Smith

Epilogue

CEF is Christians Engaged in Faith Formation. If we call ourselves Christian, that's what we do. It is our biblical mandate. From Jesus's command to "make disciples of all nations... and teaching them to obey everything that I have commanded you," (MT 28: 19, 20) to "teach what is consistent with sound doctrine...and in your teaching show integrity," (Titus 2: 1, 6) and many other scriptures, we are called to share the Good News. We are to help people grow up into the mind of Christ (1 Corinthians 2:16). We "are being transformed... from one degree of glory to another, for this comes from the Lord, the Spirit" (2 Corinthians 3:18).

The cover image of the potter reminds us of the prophecy about the potter and clay in Jeremiah 18. God, the Potter, molds and forms us into what we can be. The process is messy and takes time. It is a good metaphor to describe what all Faith Formers do. Each one is a potter. We work with the Master Potter who continues to form us as we continue to help others.

Since disciples first started following Jesus and hopefully long into the future, people have continued to learn and teach. This book is a small collection of people to whom we are most grateful: parents, grandparents, teachers, pastors, professors, writers and researchers. We are part of an ongoing parade of witnesses to the Good News.

There are many Faith Formers not featured in this book that have had significant influence on the organization of CEF in general and in particular. R. Harold Hipps and his colleagues planted the seeds for what became CEF. People such as James Fowler, Dorothy Jean Furnish, Doug Wingeier, Mary Elizabeth and Allen Moore, Walter Brueggemann, Taylor and June McConnell, Calvin Dale McConnell, and so many more. Readers surely must wonder why some persons were left out of this collection. The answer is simple: Essays were not submitted in the 15 months that the current CEF board put out invitations to submit, so the story is incomplete and ongoing.

May each one be an intentional faith former, a disciple making disciples for Jesus Christ to the honor and glory of the Holy Three in One and One in Three.

Acknowledgements

The CEF Board of Directors gratefully acknowledges all the contributors to this volume as well as the many persons who have formed our faith as individuals and as a board. While a lot of hard work has gone into this book, we acknowledge that it is only a snapshot of the many unsung heroes. We acknowledge that the church and world needs more people like them.

Every effort has been made to accurately bring to print the work of all the contributors, we acknowledge and ask forgiveness for errors contained herein.

The photos that appear in the book were provided by the writers, family members, or are in public domain.

To the 2018 Conference Design Team, the board offers its hearty appreciation for all its work on this special 50th anniversary of CEF.

To David and Joy Melton and the rest of the 50th anniversary celebration team, many thanks for all of your work.

To all the Faith Formers everywhere, you are the reason that we have hope, you are witnesses to the truth that "love wins" and the Good News of Jesus Christ will continue to shape the world.

If you would like to know more about CEF, please see the website: www.cefumc.org. We are also on Face book and Twitter.

Christians Engaged
in Faith Formation

"They devoted themselves to the apostles' teaching and fellowship in the breaking of bread and the prayers."

— Acts 2:42

Index of Contributors

Ed. Note: Each of the contributors wrote or gave interviews and permission for their essays to be used and edited in this.

Index of Photographs

1. Eugene M. Anderson quoted in *Mentoring in Religious Education* by Leona M. English (Religious Education Press: Birmingham, 1998), 6.

Scott Hughes

Author's/Editor's Biography

The Rev. Dr. Patty Meyers is Professor of Christian Education and Church Music at Pfeiffer University. A deacon in full connection with the Oregon-Idaho Annual Conference, she is a certified Director of Christian Education and Music and been in professional ministry in The United Methodist Church for 38 years. She is the current President of Christians Engaged in Faith Formation (CEF).

She is well-known in The United Methodist Church for taking more than 150 Pfeiffer undergraduates to CEF conferences, helping them network with potential employers or internship supervisors. She started the Pfeiffer chapter of CEF in 2002, which continues to this day. They lead worship particularly in small membership congregations. Three current Pfeiffer students will present workshops at the 2018 CEF Conference in October. She is a past president of United Methodist Scholars in Christian Education and has served on many conference boards and agencies in the denomination.

Dr. Meyers has served the Church in numerous ways. She has written dozens of books, articles, songs and curricula for persons of all ages. She has been a keynote speaker and workshop facilitator throughout the Church. Among the awards she has received are Outstanding Professor at Marylhurst University in Oregon and the Exemplary Teacher Award at Pfeiffer University.

Dr. Meyers holds the following academic degrees: Doctorate in Educational Leadership, Doctorate in Applied

Ministries in Religious Education, Master of Arts in Christian Education and Bachelor of Music. One of Dr. Meyers' legacies is Pfeiffer's Sports Ministry program, which she started ten years ago. In addition to teaching full time at Pfeiffer, she does music ministries at First United Methodist Church of Landis in Western North Carolina Conference.

She and husband Bob have a "four-legged child" at home, their Chihuahua, Tacy. Their daughters and families all live in Idaho. Her hobbies include reading, playing the piano, knitting and tennis. You can join her walking the beach on the Oregon Coast after the 2018 CEF Conference.